Bargaining for Competitiveness

Law, Research, and Case Studies

Bargaining for Competitiveness

Law, Research, and Case Studies

Richard N. Block
Editor

2003

W.E. Upjohn Institute for Employment Research
Kalamazoo, Michigan

Library of Congress Cataloging-in-Publication Data

Bargaining for competitiveness : law, research, and case studies /
Richard N. Block, editor.
    p. cm.
Includes bibliographical references and index.
    ISBN 0-88099-261-1 (pbk. : alk. paper) — ISBN 0-88099-262-X
(hardcover : alk. paper)
    1. Collective bargaining—United States. 2. Collective
bargaining—European Union countries. 3. Job security—United States.
4. Job security—European Union countries. 5. Labor unions—Law and
legislation—United States. 6. Labor unions—Law and
legislation—European Union countries. 7. Wages and labor productivity.
8. Labor economics. 9. Competition, International. 10.
Globalization—Economic aspects. 11. Comparative industrial relations.
I. Block, Richard N. II. W.E. Upjohn Institute for Employment Research.
    HD6508.B357 2003
    331.89'0973—dc21

                              2003004639

© 2003

W.E. Upjohn Institute for Employment Research
300 S. Westnedge Avenue
Kalamazoo, Michigan 49007–4686

The facts presented in this study and the observations and viewpoints expressed are
the sole responsibility of the authors. They do not necessarily represent positions of
the W.E. Upjohn Institute for Employment Research.

Cover design by Alcorn Publication Design.
Index prepared by Nancy Humphreys.
Printed in the United States of America.
Printed on recycled paper.

Dedication

To Marcia, Talia, Jessica, Henry, Ferne, Marty, Harriet, and Anita.

Contents

Figures

Tables

Preface

This book has its roots in a late 1990s project initiated by the International Labor Organization in Geneva. The purpose of the project was to answer, for 15 industrialized countries, a simple question: was collective bargaining compatible with firm competitiveness and employment? The standard neoclassical response was that, in the long run, they were incompatible, especially if competitors were not required to engage in collective bargaining. The broader question implicit in the study was whether an industrialized society could provide its workers a level of industrial democracy without compromising the society's interest in the efficient production of goods and services.

Equally important was the question of employment. The standard neoclassical model suggests that unionization and collective bargaining will reduce employment in the unionized sector, as unionized firms see a drop in the demand for their goods due to relatively high prices and are encouraged to substitute capital for relatively high-wage unionized labor. If this occurs, wage rates in the non-union sector drop as formerly unionized workers bid down non-union wage rates, and the burden on society is increased because these formerly unionized employees are unable to find jobs. Thus, the notion was that collective bargaining was incompatible with increasing employment.

The editor of this volume was asked to do the U.S. segment of the project, which was completed in late 1999. Each of the studies was to follow a uniform template: a detailed review of the literature on collective bargaining, employment, and competitiveness, three to five case studies, and a conclusion.

The ILO was unable to publish the 15-country study. Despite this ILO decision, however, the editor believed that the lessons of the U.S. component of the study would be valuable for the industrial relations community in the United States. The review of the literature, it was believed, would be useful for policymakers and researchers in industrial relations, and the case studies could be a valuable learning aid for students, as well as provide insight into plant- or site-level industrial relations for academics, policymakers, and practitioners. The editor approached the W.E. Upjohn Institute for Employment Research, who expressed an interest in publishing the U.S. segment.

For the Upjohn book, freed from the length constraints of the ILO research, we made some changes in the basic ILO work. An introductory chapter was added to place the U.S. system of industrial relations in an international context. The review of the literature was divided into chapters, now Chapter 2 on the legal framework for collective bargaining, competitiveness, and employment, and Chapter 3 reviewing the economics and industrial relations research on collective bargaining, competitiveness, and employment.

Chapter 4 was added to explain the methodology used. The case studies, Chapters 5–8, were strengthened to add additional economic context for the individual bargaining relationships. Chapter 9, the conclusions, was also lengthened. Overall, we hope the book accomplishes its goal of providing useful information on the U.S. collective bargaining system.

A volume such as this requires the support of many people. Professor Thomas Kochan of Massachusetts Institute of Technology, Betty Barrett, now with Massachusetts Institute of Technology, and Peggy Kelly, Muneto Ozaki, and Zafar Shaheed, all of the ILO, were essential to the research. Kevin Hollenbeck, Rich Wyrwa, and Allison Colosky, all of the W.E. Upjohn Institute for Employment Research, also provided their expertise and assistance.

Most important, however, the editors and chapter authors wish to thank the many people in the participating organizations who provided us with access for the case studies. This work could not have been done without them. They are as follows, listed alphabetically within their respective organizations: Alcoa—Dennis Carney, Joe Cleveland, Jon Cook, Matt Everitt, Greg Freehling, Jim Michaud, and Bob Turner. United Steelworkers of America Local 4895—Lloyd Anders, Bill Eckert, Larry Nolen, Stephen Srnensky. General Motors–Lansing—John Couthen Jr., Matthew Boyle, Michael Reinerth, and William Scheffler. UAW Local 652—Ralph Sheppard, Art Baker, and Fred Charles. Lear Corporation–Elsie—David Chambers, Stan Jablowski, Julie Laxton. UAW Local 1660—Christopher Jordan, Terry Clatt, Linda Rathbun, Jack Tyler. Sparrow Health Systems—Ollie Aldridge, Kim Alexander, Debbie Barron, Evelyn Bochenek, Chris Marin, George Maier, Gary McMillan, Dan Phillips, Fran Sklapsky, Shirley Stephenson, and Pam Tilton. Professional Employees Council of Sparrow Hospital/Michigan Nurses Association—Lori Certo, Catherine Dunn, Patricia Frye, Diane Goddeeris, Gail Jehl, Judy McLane, Terri Peaphon, and Jesusa Vasquez. Sparrow/PECSH Mutual Gains Committee—Mary Ann Daly, Kim Ford, Jim Fischer, Ira Ginsburg, Gail Grannell, Kathy Kacynski, John Karebian, Rita Michaels, Renee Rivard, Gordon Taylor, and Fred Vocino.

1

Collective Bargaining in Context

Comparing the United States and Europe

Richard N. Block
Peter Berg
Michigan State University

This book is an analysis of the relationship among collective bargaining, firm competitiveness, and employment protection/creation in the United States. Collective bargaining, at its essence, is the determination of terms and conditions of employment through negotiation between an employer and a representative of the employer's employees acting collectively as a group; hence the term collective bargaining. Although collective bargaining is generally contrasted with individual bargaining, for the vast majority of employees in the United States, the alternative to collective bargaining is unilateral determination of terms and conditions of employment by the employer, with perhaps a small zone of negotiations over wages or salaries and/or job duties.

Few institutions in the United States generate as much continuing controversy as collective bargaining. Any attempt to change the laws surrounding collective bargaining brings out waves of lobbyists, often attempting to invoke deep value-laden arguments to advocate or oppose legislative changes that serve or disserve the interests of unions and employers (Block 1997). For those who favor collective bargaining, unions and collective bargaining are an indispensable element of a democratic society. Unionism and collective bargaining provide industrial democracy, a means by which employees have a voice in their workplace lives. Only through the power associated with collective representation can employees make that voice heard. They argue that to be effective, such collective representation requires, at times, a willingness to subordinate the interests of the individual worker to the interests of the collectivity of workers. They would disagree that unions and collective bargaining impair economic efficiency, arguing that in some circumstances unions enhance efficiency, and that the theoretical inefficiency argument incorporates a set of competitiveness assumptions that rarely hold. Moreover, proponents of collective bargaining would argue that even if unions impair economic efficiency, it is only short-run impairment that disappears after employers make adjustments in employment practices and production processes in response to unionism (Block 1995).

On the other hand, while those on the other side of the debate do not, in principle, oppose voluntary unionism, they would argue, as noted, that legally protected unionism and collective bargaining result in economic and political distortions that are inconsistent with efficiency and democracy. Collective bargaining, it is argued, gives disproportionate labor market power to employees, resulting in higher wages to unionized workers (e.g., supercompetitive wages) than they would receive in a competitive labor market in the absence of collective bargaining. Unionism also results in lower employment in the unionized sector than would otherwise occur, as the high unionized wages and terms and conditions of employment discourage employers from hiring workers. This low employment in the unionized sector causes unemployed workers to shift to the non-union sector, resulting in excess labor supply and lower wages for those workers. Thus, as compared to a competitive labor market, the distortionary effects associated with collective bargaining include lower employment for unionized workers, lower wages for nonunion workers, lower profits for shareholders, and less investment and economic growth.

Politically, to the extent that unionism requires the subordination of the interests of individual employees to a larger group, or collectivity of employees, it can be seen as inconsistent with individual rights. In addition, by forcing employers to negotiate with the employees' representative over matters affecting employment, collective bargaining impairs the property rights of employers to allocate their resources in the way that they see fit.

Despite concerns raised by skeptics of unionism and collective bargaining, all developed, industrialized, democratic countries have created collective bargaining systems (U.S. Department of State 1999). The values underlying these systems, however, differ across countries, reflecting, to a greater or lesser extent, the views expressed above. Although this book focuses solely on collective bargaining in the

United States, in a world of globalization, a complete understanding of the U.S. collective bargaining system involves placing the system in a worldwide context. This is best done by comparing the values underlying the collective bargaining system in the United States with values underlying the collective bargaining systems in other industrialized countries; we discuss this in the next section of this chapter. The following section undertakes a similar examination of Europe as an example of industrialized democracies with collective bargaining systems exhibiting a different set of values. The final section provides a summary.

VALUES AND EMPLOYMENT IN THE UNITED STATES

As noted, collective bargaining may be defined as the establishment of terms and conditions of the employment relationship through negotiation between an employer and a (legally recognized) representative of the employer's employees acting collectively as a group. There are two key elements to collective bargaining: the collectivization of employees and the employment relationship. In the United States, both of these elements are associated with certain values, premises, or assumptions that determine the status of collective bargaining. These values and assumptions are so ingrained in U.S. culture that it may be difficult to recognize them as values or assumptions that may not be universally accepted. Nevertheless, they do define how collective bargaining is viewed in the United States. Each of these elements will be examined through the lens of values.

Collectivism and the Employment Relationship

In the United States, a very high value has traditionally been placed on individualism. Indeed, as has been observed in a study of individualism and life in the United States, "individualism lies at the very core of American culture" (Bellah et al. 1987, p. 142).

In the context of collectivizing the employment relationship, the primacy of individualism means that the rights of individuals are gen-

erally superior to other rights, and that individual rights take prece-
dence over other rights when there is a perceived conflict.

American culture views the exercise of property rights as a direct
derivative of individual rights. The basic principle is that individuals
should be free to use and dispose of their property as they see fit, so
long as no laws are violated. In other words, freedom of contract is
highly valued. Individuals should be free to pursue their economic
interests, generally free from restraints.[1]

While one can readily conceive of people possessing individual
rights, corporations have generally been viewed as legal individuals,
with, for the most part, the same panoply of individual rights possessed
by persons. Thus, corporations, which are fundamentally voluntary
collectivities of shareholders, may pursue their individual (corporate)
interests with the same vigor as persons.

As a result, the terms and conditions of the typical employment
relationship are established by the agreement of two individuals, the
employee and the corporation/employer, each exercising individual
rights to obtain a mutually agreeable bargain that is in their respective
interests, although neither party can include terms or conditions of
employment that are illegal. Indeed, this individual determination of
the terms and conditions of employment is the "default" or "normal"
process in the United States for establishing the terms and conditions
of employment.

Operating in such a milieu, unions, as collectivities of employees,
are at a cultural disadvantage. Collectively determined terms and conditions of employment are considered the exception to the "normal"
process of individual determination. Collectivization occurs only if a
majority of the employees in *unit* decide to collectivize the relationship
through the established legal procedures. Even if the employees decide
to collectivize, the choice may be rescinded at appropriate times (Hardin and Higgins 2001).

Over the years, there has been a great deal of legal debate and posi-
tioning, both legislatively and before legal tribunals, regarding the
proper scope of collective activity. This is because in order to act as an
effective collectivity and as a representative of all employees, a union
must necessarily aggregate the interests of all employees into a unified
position. This aggregation means that some employees may view
themselves as disadvantaged vis-à-vis the terms and conditions of

employment (that are perceived to be) available to them in the absence of collectivization. The point is that on occasion, the union must subordinate the interests of the individual to the interests of larger group. In addition, because of an obligation to negotiate with a union, the collective bargaining process places constraints on employer use of its property.

The result is that unionism and collective bargaining often conflict with two legal principles: individual employee rights and employer property rights. With respect to individual employee rights, although unions have been granted some privileges to pursue collective interests, there are some constraints on union behavior in circumstances in which such behavior may be viewed as being inconsistent with individual rights, as U.S. labor policy attempts to find a balance between collective action and individual rights that is consistent with its values. Thus, on the collectivity end of the continuum, a union, when chosen as the legal bargaining representative, represents all employees in the unit, and no employee may agree with the employer on terms and conditions of employment that are inconsistent with those on which the employer and the union have agreed. The union and the employer are also authorized to negotiate a union security clause, by which the employee must become a union member or at least pay dues and fees equal to those paid by a member. A union may also compel a member to follow its internal rules, including rules associated with working during a duly authorized strike.

On the individualism end of the continuum, as noted, a union shop provision may not compel union membership and adherence to the union's internal rules; it may compel only monetary payments. Moreover, those payments may be reduced by an amount that goes to political or non–collective bargaining activities of the union. Finally, states have the right to prohibit such provisions. Unions may not limit the rights of persons to resign from the union, thus constraining the extent to which working during a strike can be restrained. Unions may not use dues and fees collected under a union security clause for political purposes, as such use might be viewed as inconsistent with the employee's freedom of speech and association.

The conflict between employee collective activity and employer property rights has also been an attempt to strike a proper balance. On the employee collectivity end of the continuum, employees have the right to engage in organizational activity at the workplace on nonwork time, and the employer must negotiate over terms and conditions of employment with a union representing the employees. On the property rights end of the continuum, the employer may generally prohibit a union (distinct from employees) from organizing on its property and may oppose a union organizational attempt by legal means. An employer may also make major changes in the structure of its business without negotiating with the union over those changes.

The Employment Relationship

In the United States, the employment relationship has always been viewed as primarily an economic transaction rather than a relationship that incorporates social content. This view is exemplified by the adherence of the United States to the doctrine of employment-at-will: as a general principle, either party can terminate the employment relationship at any time. In other words, the employment relationship is value-based; it exists only so long as that relationship creates sufficient value for both the employer and the employee. When the value created is insufficient for just one of the parties, the relationship can be terminated with no required notice.[2]

It is also telling that there are few legal or societal requirements associated with the level of terms and conditions of employment. With the exception of the substantive requirements to pay a minimum wage and overtime for certain employees who work more than 40 hours in a week or 80 hours over two weeks, the bulk of U.S. employment policy, embodied in law, generally addresses only discrimination and differential treatment as between groups of employees viewed as being favored and employees in "protected groups." Thus, there is no law requiring that employers provide health insurance for employees. But the law does prohibit employers who choose to provide health insurance from providing greater levels of coverage for males than for females, for example. The law does not state the wage the employer must pay, but the law prohibits an employer from paying female employees less than male employees, and vice versa.[3]

This principle of nondiscrimination is consistent with the values the United States places on individualism and productivity. As a general rule, employees should be hired and rewarded based not on immutable characteristics, but rather on business considerations and the value they create. Thus, employment policy is not truly designed to address social concerns. Rather, it is designed to ensure that the labor market functions efficiently, with employment-related decisions based on productivity rather than personal characteristics unrelated to value.

VALUES AND EMPLOYMENT IN EUROPE

With a market that rivals the size of the United States, the European Union (EU) is a dominant force in the global economy. Moreover, with the recent monetary union and eventual expansion into eastern Europe in the next five years, the EU will play an increasingly important role in the industrialized economies. As a confederation of nations, the political and regulatory frameworks within the EU differ across countries. Some countries reflect market liberalism and a laissez-faire approach to regulation, while others emphasize a collectivist or corporatist approach to policy (Leat 1998). Despite these differences in regulatory orientation, the European Commission has actively sought to harmonize labor standards across member states. Harmonizing labor standards through the policy-making process and the binding directives from the European Commission have a significant impact on the rights of employees on issues of participation, employment security, and collective bargaining across European countries. Moreover, the values behind these standards reflect a different approach to collectivism and individualism and the employment relationship when compared with the United States. In this section, we contrast the values in Europe regarding collectivism and the employment relationship with those of the United States discussed previously.

Collectivism and the Employment Relationship

In the United States, individual employees are given the right to form a labor union or collective body to represent them at the workplace. The existence of labor unions comes from the desire of individuals who vote to form or disband them. Labor unions have no legal status at the workplace apart from that given to them by individual employees. In addition, their role in society is largely economic. They represent workers in their negotiations with companies about wages and working conditions.

Although labor unions engage in political activity in the United States, they are viewed no differently in the political process than any other interest group. Labor unions in the United States are not given special roles in policy making and are not perceived as serving a social function.

In contrast, collective organizations in Europe are afforded rights apart from individuals and are given explicit roles as representative organizations in EU policy making. In Germany, they are given rights in the constitution to exist and carry out activities that serve their underlying purposes (Berghahn and Karsten 1987). In addition, labor unions across Europe do not have to win elections in order to exist or negotiate with management. Labor unions in many European countries often negotiate with employer associations in centralized bargaining structures where contracts are extended to workers in all firms within the employer association. Labor unions in some European countries serve quasi-public roles. For example, in Sweden and Belgium, labor unions manage the unemployment insurance system (Visser 1996). In France, labor unions manage a number of social security funds, including unemployment benefits and work accident insurance (Graham 2000). Moreover, in Germany, labor unions participate with employer associations in determining the curriculum for various occupations in the German system of vocational training (Berg 1994).

Reflecting the role played by labor unions and employer associations within member countries, the EU has integrated the input of labor and employer peak associations into the policy-making structure of the EU. Prior to instituting directives, the European Commission consults with labor and employer representatives in an effort to build consensus. Social directives that affect the employment relationship, such as working time or part-time work, will come into effect only after a negotiated consensus emerges with labor and employer representatives. This approach to policy making reflects the value attached to consensus, consultation, and corporatism within Europe and the European Union (Sciarra 1999).

The key point regarding the discussion above reflects the fundamental differences in the views of unionism between the United States and the EU. Whereas labor unions in the United States are viewed as having a strictly economic function, labor unions and employer associations in Europe are commonly referred to as *social partners*. These partners are engaged in a social dialogue within a social market economy. The word *partners* implies equality between labor and employers in the employment relationship. While the bargaining power between the two may not always be equal, the term *social partners* describes how both labor and employers are seen as having equal legitimacy within the society. The explicit recognition that the European economy is a social market economy rather than simply a market economy is reflective of how the employment relationship is viewed in Europe.

The Employment Relationship

Unlike the United States, which gives virtually total authority to property owners or shareholders over business and investment decisions, governments in Europe are much more willing to support the rights of stakeholders, such as labor unions and workers, to a say in business and employment-related decisions. For example, in Germany employees have the opportunity to elect a works council that has rights to information, consultation, and codetermination on various employment-related issues. Management must consult with works councils on issues regarding personnel planning, such as implementing new technology or changing the organization of work. However, on issues of pay schemes or work schedules, management and the works council must codetermine the policy. Similar rights of participation exist in the Netherlands, Sweden, Belgium, France, Denmark, Austria, and Switzerland.

Recognizing that these national rights to participation and consultation can be diminished in a global economy where relevant corporate decisions fall outside their jurisdiction, the EU implemented a European-wide works council directive in 1994 and later extended its coverage to include more countries in 1997. The European Works Councils (EWCs) are established within large, multinational companies operating in Europe. These councils do not give employees or trade unions the same extensive rights to codetermination enjoyed by workers in national legislation. Instead, EWCs' main objective is to provide employees with information and allow for consultation with management. The establishment of EWCs by the EU illustrates its willingness to support the rights of stakeholders to have a voice in the employment relationship between workers and companies operating in Europe. The European Works Council Directive also shows the types of labor and social standards the EU wants to harmonize across countries. With monetary union bringing countries closer together, greater harmonization of labor and social standards is likely to follow.

The EU is also strengthening the role of collective bargaining in the implementation of European legislation. European Union directives often use collective bargaining as an instrument of flexibility. Directives regarding health and safety and working time use collective bargaining as a means of negotiating flexibility into broad multinational legislation (Veneziani 1999).

SUMMARY

Rather than provide the reader with a full description of collective bargaining in the United States, the discussion in this chapter is intended to demonstrate that the assumptions underlying work, employment, and employee collectivism in the United States are value-based conceptions of employment rather than universally recognized truths. United States culture values individualism, property rights, and a transaction view of employment, and that is reflected in American conceptions of employment and the narrow and circumspect role of collective bargaining and unionism in the employment relations system. On the other hand, European culture values collectivism more than the United States culture, and Europe is more willing than the United States to see employment as having a social purpose as well as an economic purpose. Thus, unions and collective bargaining play a much greater role in the European employment system than in the United States employment system.

Thus, as one reads the case studies in this volume, one should understand that they reflect the U.S. collective bargaining system and U.S. conceptions of employment. Moreover, we will better understand the collective bargaining system in the United States when we realize that there are other systems in industrialized democracies with a different set of values and assumptions.

Notes

This research was supported in part by the International Labor Organization under contract no. 5453. The views expressed in this book are those of the authors and do not necessarily reflect the views of the International Labor Organization.

1. Freedom of contract is limited, as there are some "contracts" that the United States has determined are sufficiently undesirable as to be unlawful. Thus, an employer and an employee may not agree to pay a wage below the legal minimum, even if the employee would accept such a wage.
2. In economic terms, the value of the employment relationship will be sufficient for the employer to maintain it when the employee's marginal revenue product, the additional revenue produced from an additional unit (hour) of that employee's labor is at least sufficient to cover the employee's compensation. For the employee, the value of the employment relationship will be sufficient to maintain it when the employee's compensation is at least equal to his or her reservation wage, or the minimum level of compensation the employee must receive to keep the job. The reservation wage is influenced by such factors as fixed expenses associated with employment (e.g., commuting, child care) and by the wage rate the employee could obtain with another employer.
3. In contrast, there is no law prohibiting employers from discriminating against workers on the basis of employment status. Thus, full- and part-time workers performing the same work can be paid differently.

References

Bellah, Robert N., Richard Madsen, William M. Sullivan, Ann Swidler, and Steven M. Tipton. 1987. *Habits of the Heart: Individualism and Commitment in American Life*. Berkeley, California, Los Angeles, California, London, UK: University of California Press.

Berg, Peter. 1994. "The German Training System." In *Britain's Training Deficit: The Centre for Economic Performance Report*, Richard Layard, Ken Mayhew, and Geoffrey Owen, eds. Aldershot, Great Britain: Avebury Press, pp. 282–308.

Berghahn, Volker R., and Detlev Karsten. 1987. *Industrial Relations in West Germany*. New York: Berg Publishers.

Block, Richard N. 1995. "Labor Law, Economics, and Industrial Democracy: A Reconciliation." *Industrial Relations* 34(3): 402–416.

————. 1997. "Rethinking the National Labor Relations Act and Zero-Sum Labor Law: An Industrial Relations View." *Berkeley Journal of Labor and Employment Law* 18(1): 30–55.

Graham, Robert. 2000. "French Employers to Decide on 35-Hour Battle." *Financial Times*, January 18.

Hardin, Patrick, and John C. Higgins Jr. 2001. *The Developing Labor Law*, 4th ed. Washington, DC: Bureau of National Affairs.

Leat, Mike. 1998. *Human Resources Issues of the European Union*. London, Washington, DC: Financial Times Management.

Sciarra, Silvana. 1999. "The Employment Title in the Amsterdam Treaty: A Multi-Language Discourse." In *Legal Issues of the Amsterdam Treaty,* David O'Keefe and Patrick Twomey, eds. Oxford, and Portland, Oregon: Hart Publishing, pp. 157–170.

U.S. Department of Stat. 1999. *1999 Country Reports On Economic Policy and Trade Practices.* Washington, DC: Bureau of Economic and Business Affairs.

Visser, Jelle. 1996. "Corporatism beyond Repair? Industrial Relations in Sweden." In *Industrial Relations in Europe,* Joris Van Ruysseveldt and Jelle Visser, eds. London: Sage Publications, pp. 175–204.

Veneziani, Bruno. 1999. "The Intervention of the Law to Regulate Collective Bargaining and Trade Union Representation Rights in European Countries: Recent Trends and Problems." *Transfer* 5(1–2): 100–135.

2

Competitiveness and Employment Protection and Creation

An Overview of Collective Bargaining in the United States

Richard N. Block
Michigan State University

A discussion of the relationship between collective bargaining, competitiveness, and employment protection and creation in the United States can be undertaken only in the context of a thorough understanding of the institutions governing and affecting the collective bargaining in the United States. There is no actor, institution, or subsystem in the United States that encourages the collective bargaining system to be used for those—or any—purposes. Public policy in the United States neither encourages nor discourages collective bargaining as a method of establishing terms and conditions of employment. Rather, public policy is designed to protect the choice of employees as to whether they wish to be represented by a union or labor organization for the purposes of collective bargaining.[1]

When employees are represented for collective bargaining purposes by a union, there is no government involvement in establishing the outcomes of bargaining. As a result, the major characteristic of the U.S. collective bargaining system is variation. From the viewpoint of firms, competitiveness can be obtained through collective bargaining or through other mechanisms. Put differently, there may be multiple paths to competitiveness for a firm, and the collective bargaining system is but one of those paths.

The main purpose of this overview is to explore the nature of the collective bargaining environment in the United States as it relates to the use of the collective bargaining system for encouraging competitiveness and employment protection/creation. To that end, the next section will explore that environment. The third section will present a brief overview of some of the literature on the incidence of the use of the collective bargaining system in the United States as a vehicle for competitiveness and employment protection/creation. The final section will present a summary and conclusions.

THE ENVIRONMENT FOR COLLECTIVE BARGAINING, COMPETITIVENESS, AND EMPLOYMENT PROTECTION/CREATION

Collective bargaining by individual firms and unions, which affects competitiveness and employment protection/creation, is heavily influenced by the environments in which the labor relations system must exist. Indeed, there are several environments that exert an impact on the relationship between collective bargaining for competitiveness and employment protection/creation. These environments associated with collective bargaining include the legal, political, institutional, and economic. Each of these will be examined.

The Legal Environment

By far the most important influence on the collective bargaining system in the United States is the law; in this case, the National Labor Relations Act (NLRA) as amended in 1947 and then again in 1959. The law establishes the overall framework for the collective bargaining system in the United States. The influence and reach of the law derives from the fact that it is accessible, covers almost all firms in the private sector outside of the railroad and airline industries, and is public. The law's accessibility means that all have access to its process. Its broad coverage results in a broad application, and its public nature means that the decisions that emanate from it are known by the labor relations community and can be used to influence other decisions and shape new legal arguments. Therefore, parties acting through their attorneys have a common information base on what is illegal, what is legal, and what is debatable.

The law establishes the basic structure for collective bargaining, the procedural obligations of parties to negotiate, and the matters about which they must negotiate. Equally important, it establishes the parameters within which government may intercede in the bargaining process to encourage the parties to negotiate substantive terms or conditions of employment, such as those that influence competitiveness and employment protection/creation.

Historical Overview of Labor Law in the United States

The basic legislation governing labor relations in the United States, the NLRA, was enacted in 1935. Although the purposes of the act have been the subject of much debate (Keyserling 1945; Millis and Brown 1950; Block 1995, 1997), one obvious reason for the passage of the law was to create an orderly process for determining whether a group of employees wished to be represented by a union for collective purposes.

An important assumption underlying the U.S. industrial relations system was reflected in this basic purpose. Employees would only be represented by a union if they wished to be so represented. Collective bargaining and union representation were not presumed to be the method by which terms and conditions of employment were normally established. Rather, such terms and conditions of employment were normally established by the employer unilaterally or by individual employer negotiation with employees.

The 1935 act also established the concept of a *bargaining unit*. The National Labor Relations Board (NLRB), the agency established to administer the NLRA, was given the responsibility to determine if any unit (such as a group of employees) was appropriate for bargaining, and if so, whether the employees in that unit desire representation. A bargaining unit could only be an "employer unit, craft unit, plant unit, or subdivision thereof" (NLRA, Sec. 9(a)). In order to be considered appropriate, the employees being considered for union representation were required to have a "community of interest," common employment interests such as similar wage structure, similar tasks, and similar supervision.

In its early years, the NLRB used card checks to determine if the employees in an appropriate bargaining unit desired union representation. The board agent would match signed union cards to a list of employees provided by the employer. By the early 1940s, the board had established the representation election as the preferred method of determining representation (Millis and Brown 1950). Thus, by the early 1940s, the bargaining unit could accurately be labeled an *election unit*, which would be a bargaining unit only if the employees in that unit chose a union to represent them for collective purposes.

Union representation would exist only if a majority of the employees desired to be so represented. Moreover, as the law would later evolve, it would also be determined that the desire for unionization must be continuing. Thus, if a majority of the employees in a bargaining unit at some point decided that they no longer wished union representation, such representation would be ended.

The result is that the legal structure in the United States creates a unit-by-unit, workplace-by-workplace process for unionization and, as will be seen, for bargaining. Moreover, once union representation is established in a unit, the employer has an obligation to bargain only with the union representing the employees in that unit. There is no obligation to bargain with any other union or labor organization for employees not in that unit, and the union or labor organization may not negotiate for employees who are outside that unit unless those other employees are represented by a union and agree to so negotiate, the employees are added (accreted) to the existing bargaining unit through a legal proceeding, or the employer agrees to negotiate with an existing union for those employees and, if challenged, all legal standards for unit accretion are met.

The NLRA was extensively amended in 1947 via the Taft-Hartley Act. For the purpose of this study, the 1947 amendments changed the 1935 law in three key ways. First, the 1947 amendments established the representation election as the preferred method of determining whether a unit of employees wished to be represented by a union. Consistent with this preference, card checks would only be used under extraordinary circumstances, such as when a fair election was impossible due to the employer's extensive unfair labor practices (*NLRB v. Gissel Packing Co.*, 395 U.S. 575 [1969]). Second, the 1947 amendments gave employers rights of free speech. Thereafter, employer expressions of sentiment against unionization would not be viewed as unlawful unless accompanied by a direct or implied threat of job loss or promise of benefit. Third, the Taft-Hartley amendments refined the obligation of the employer to bargain with the union by providing that the parties were required to meet at reasonable times and to discuss matters related to terms and conditions of employment. On the other hand, the amendment provided that neither party had an obligation to agree to any proposal. As will be discussed below, these three changes would have an impact on bargaining for competitiveness and employment protection/creation (Millis and Brown 1950; Block, Beck, and Kruger 1996).

Lesser amendments to the NLRA were enacted in 1958 and 1974. The 1958 amendments are relevant to this study only to the extent that they placed some limitations on the rights of unions to engage in recognized organizational picketing. The 1974 amendments brought employees of nonprofit, private health care institutions under the NLRA.[2]

Law and Bargaining Structure

One result of the system of establishing union representation on a unit-by-unit basis is the absence of an overarching structure for collective bargaining. Because the legal bargaining units are the basic building blocks of the collective bargaining system, the result has been the creation of a highly decentralized system of collective bargaining in the United Sates based on the plant-by-plant, unit-by-unit certification process. Each legal bargaining unit negotiates terms and conditions of employment only for those employees in the bargaining unit unless all affected parties explicitly and unambiguously agree to a more inclusive bargaining structure. Even when such an inclusive bargaining structure exists, any or all parties can leave the multiemployer or multiunion structure at the termination of the collective agreement (Evening News Association 1965; Detroit Newspaper Agency 1998).

This unit-by-unit system of establishing bargaining is important to the relationship between collective bargaining, competitiveness, and employment protection/creation because it creates a system under which employers have substantial flexibility and discretion in making decisions regarding competitiveness. The unit-by-unit representation system and the default system of "no union" means that there is no necessary relationship between unionization in the facilities of a firm. The mere fact that one facility of an employer is unionized does not mean that other facilities of the employer are unionized. This occurs because in most cases, the bargaining or election unit is the plant/facility or sub-division thereof. Many firms have both unionized and nonunion facilities, and some firms have facilities represented by different unions. On occasion, more than one union may represent different classifications of employees in one facility.

This system gives many employers competitiveness options away from the union in addition to negotiating with the union. Alternatively, multiple unions within a firm raise the possibility of employer use of coercive comparisons, comparing the willingness of one union or local to compromise with the willingness of other unions or locals to compromise. These options can provide employers with a disincentive to compromise with unions during negotiations on matters that might be thought to enhance competitiveness and employment protection. In the alternative, these options can provide employers with leverage during negotiations. Such leverage makes it less likely than otherwise that direct employment protection or creation that would normally benefit unions will be incorporated into collective agreements. At the same time, such a situation can also provide unions with leverage over employers where the union has organized a key facility.

In general, however, cooperation occurs only if both parties are interested in cooperation. On the other hand, if one party is uninterested in cooperation, the legal system will not encourage it—in fact, it will resist it.

Law and the Bargaining Process

A central premise of collective bargaining law in the United States is government noninterference in the bargaining process. The law does require both parties to bargain in "good faith." But, as amended in 1947, the NLRA explicitly states that the obligation to bargain in good faith "does not compel either party to agree to a proposal or require the making of a concession" (NLRA as amended, Section 8(d)). As the U.S. Supreme Court noted in a key 1960 decision, commenting on the 1947 debate around legislation that would clarify the obligation to bargain in the 1935 law:

> the nature of the duty to bargain in good faith thus imposed upon employers . . . was not sweepingly conceived. The Chairman of the Senate Committee declared: "When the employees have chosen their organization, when they have selected their representa-

tives, all the bill proposes to do is to escort them to the door of their employer and say, 'Here they are, the legal representatives of your employees.' What happens behind those doors is not inquired into, and the bill does not seek to inquire into it."

The limitation implied by the last sentence has not been in practice maintained – practically, it could hardly have been – but the underlying purpose of the remark has remained the most basic purpose of the statutory provision . . . Congress was generally not concerned with the substantive terms on which the parties contracted. (*NLRB v. Insurance Agents International Union*, 361 U.S. 477 [1960, 484–487])

Legislation passed in 1947 is equally clear regarding what the parties are obligated to do in bargaining, and what they are not obligated to do.

To bargain collectively is the performance of the mutual obligation of the employer and the representative of the employees to meet at reasonable times and confer in good faith with respect to wages, hours, and other terms and conditions of employment, or the negotiation of an agreement, or any question arising thereunder, and the execution of a written contract incorporating any agreement reached if requested by either party, but such obligation does not compel either party to agree to a proposal or require the making of a concession. (NLRA, Section 8d)

United States labor law does not require either party to agree to any proposal made by the other party, including any matter regarding competitiveness and employment protection/creation. Labor law only requires each party to negotiate in good faith over matters involving terms and conditions of employment, so that parties must discuss employment protection and competitiveness, at least to the extent that competitiveness is germane to terms and conditions of employment.

Thus, labor law in the United States enables the parties to use collective bargaining to agree on issues relating to competitiveness and employment protection/creation, but only if both wish to do so. Equally important, it also enables either party not to address these issues, if that party believes that it will be better off by declining to agree, provided that the party negotiates in good faith. The NLRA is indifferent to the bargaining outcomes on matters of employment protection and competitiveness, just as it is indifferent to the outcomes on any other specific issue.

In addition to this laissez-faire approach to the subjects of bargaining, labor law provides parties a wide range of weapons to pursue their self-interest. As the Supreme Court noted:

> (I) It must be realized that collective bargaining, under a system where the government does not attempt to control the results of negotiations . . . The parties—even granting the modification of views that may come from a realization of economic interdependence—still proceed from contrary and to an extent antagonistic viewpoints and concepts of self-interest. The system has not reached the ideal of the philosophic notion that perfect understanding among people would lead to perfect agreement among them on values. The presence of economic weapons in reserve, and their actual exercise on occasion by the parties, is part and parcel of the system that the Wagner and Taft–Hartley Acts have recognized. Abstract logical analysis might find inconsistency between the command of the statute to negotiate toward an agreement in good faith and the legitimacy of the use of economic weapons, frequently having the most serious effect upon individual workers and productive enterprises, to induce one party to come to the terms desired by the other. But the truth of the matter is that at the present statutory stage of our national labor relations policy, the two factors—necessity for good-faith bargaining between parties, and the availability of economic pressure devices to each to make the other party incline to agree on one's terms— exist side by side. (*NLRB v. Insurance Agents International Union*, 361 U.S. [1960, 488–489])

This panoply of economic weapons includes strikes by unions, and lockouts and the use permanent replacements by employers (*NLRB v. MacKay Radio and Telegraph Co.*, 304 U.S. 477 [1938]; *American Shipbuilding v. NLRB*, 380 U.S. 300 [1965]; *TWA v. Independent Federation of Flight Attendants*, 489 U.S. 426 [1989]). Unions can only obtain employment protection when employers see it as in their interest to grant it, or when they are able to extract it by force. Thus, if one party wishes to resist the use of the collective bargaining process to encourage competitiveness and employment protection/creation, the law permits that party to use the weapons to do so.

Law and the Obligation to Bargain over Substantive Matters

The NLRA as amended requires employers and unions to bargain in good faith over matters involving wages, hours, and other terms and conditions of employment. In 1958, the U.S. Supreme Court decided that neither party had an obligation to bargain over matters not relating to terms or conditions of employment (*NLRB v. Wooster Division of Borg-Warner Corp.*, 356 U.S. 342 [1958]). In this case, the Court created implicitly three categories of subjects: mandatory, permissive, and unlawful. Mandatory subjects were those relating to terms and conditions of employment that the parties were required to discuss, although there was no obligation to agree. Permissive subjects were those that the parties could discuss if both parties so desired; however, neither party was under an obligation to discuss them. Unlawful subjects were not permitted to be discussed or incorporated into a collective agreement. A later decision by a lower court, permitted to stand by the Supreme Court, reinforced the distinction between mandatory and permissive subjects of bargaining by holding that one party could not force another party to negotiate over a nonmandatory item by withholding agreement on a mandatory item subject to agreement on the nonmandatory item. (*International Union of Marine Workers v. NLRB*, 320 F.2d 615, 3rd cir.; [1963])

The importance of these decisions soon became clear. Employers need only bargain over matters involving terms and conditions of employment, which, in turn, meant that they could act unilaterally in matters not involving terms and conditions of employment. There ensued extensive litigation over the type of decisions that would be considered terms and conditions of employment (*NLRB v. Adams Dairy, Inc.* 350 F.2d 108 [CA 8; 1965]; *NLRB v. Royal Plating and Polishing Co.* 350 F.2d 191 [CA 3; 1965]; *First National Maintenance Corp. v. NLRB* 452 U.S. 668 [1981]). To the extent that employers were able to use the legal system to remove matters from the category "terms and conditions of employment," their flexibility would be substantially enhanced, and they could make decisions without negotiating with a union about those decisions. On the other hand, if a matter was determined to be a "term or condition of employment," employers were required to negotiate with the union over decisions involving those matters.

The most heated legal battles were fought over decisions that were traditionally considered in the United States to be the prerogative of management, but that also had an effect on employment. In the first key post–*Borg-Warner* case, *Fibreboard v. NLRB*, 379 U.S. 203 (1964), the Supreme Court determined that the employer's decision to contract out its maintenance work that had previously been done by bargaining unit employees was a mandatory subject of bargaining. In this case, the firm had replaced its unionized employees with those of a contractor. The company had determined that it cost less to have the maintenance work done by a contractor than the bargaining unit employees, and the employer believed that the union would not agree to a contract that resulted in reduced cost.

The Court agreed with the board that this subcontracting was merely the replacement of one group of employees with another based solely on labor cost. Both groups of employees would be doing precisely the same work, under the same conditions, with the same tools. It was a mere replacement of one group of employees for another. In deciding this case, however, the Court also observed:

> The subject matter of the present dispute is well within the literal meaning of the phrase "terms and conditions of employment." A stipulation with respect to the contracting out of work performed by members of the bargaining unit might appropriately be called a 'condition of employment.' The words even more plainly cover termination of employment which, as the facts of this case indicate, necessarily results from the contracting out of work performed by members of the established bargaining unit. (379 U.S. 203, 210)

This last sentence seemed to suggest that any employer decision that resulted in the termination of employment was a mandatory subject of bargaining. On the other hand, the facts of *Fibreboard* were sufficiently narrow as to generate legal doubt regarding whether that last statement applied to any employer decision, or only to contracting out decisions similar to that taken in *Fibreboard*, the mere replacement of one group of employees with another group, with the decision to replace based solely on labor costs.

Seventeen years later, the Supreme Court appeared to adopt a position opposite to *Fibreboard* in *First National Maintenance Corporation v. NLRB*. In that case, the employer, who provided cleaning and maintenance services for commercial customers, refused to bargain with its unionized employees about a decision to withdraw from a contract at Greenpark, a nursing home. The dispute with Greenpark was solely over the size of the fee that First National Maintenance would receive. In deciding that the employer had no obligation to bargain over the decision to withdraw from its Greenpark contract, the Court observed:

> In establishing what issues must be submitted to the process of bargaining, Congress had no expectation that the elected union representative would become an equal partner in the running of the business enterprise in which the union's members are employed. Despite the deliberate open-endedness of the statutory language, there is an undeniable limit to the subjects about which bargaining must take place: . . .

> (The Employer) contends it had no duty to bargain about its decision to terminate its operations at Greenpark. This contention requires that we determine whether the decision itself should be considered part of petitioner's retained freedom to manage its affairs unrelated to employment. The aim of . . . labeling a matter a mandatory subject of bargaining, rather than simply permitting, but not requiring, bargaining, is to "promote the fundamental purpose of the Act by bringing a problem of vital concern to labor and management within the framework established by Congress as most conducive to industrial peace," . . . The concept of mandatory bargaining is premised on the belief that collective discussions backed by the parties' economic weapons will result in decisions that are better for both management and labor and for society as a whole . . . This will be true, however, only if the subject proposed for discussion is amenable to resolution through the bargaining process. Management must be free from the constraints of the bargaining process . . . to the extent essential for the running of a profitable business. It also must have some degree of certainty beforehand as to when it may proceed to reach decisions without fear of later evaluations labeling its conduct an unfair labor practice. Congress did not explicitly state what issues of mutual concern to union and management it intended to exclude from mandatory bargaining. Nonetheless, in view of an employer's need for unencumbered decision making, bargaining over management decisions that have a substantial impact on the

continued availability of employment should be required only if the benefit, for labor–management relations and the collective-bargaining process, outweighs the burden placed on the conduct of the business. (452 U.S. 666, 674–679)

In other words, if the employer believed that its competitive interests, the conduct of business, would be impaired by a requirement that it must bargain with the union over the decision, and it prevailed in the legal system, there would be no bargaining obligation. In the First National Maintenance view of bargaining, collective bargaining is not necessarily a vehicle that can be used by a firm to attain competitiveness. Bargaining is just as frequently a barrier to firm competitiveness. In this view, competitiveness is solely a management interest, rather than a joint interest of management and the union.

In deciding *First National Maintenance*, the Court determined that all management decisions could be characterized as one of three types with respect to bargaining: type I, decisions that had a substantial effect on the employer but only a minimal effect or indirect effect on the employment interests of employees (e.g., pricing, financing, advertising); type II, decisions that affected solely employment (e.g., wages, working hours, benefits); and type III, decisions that had a substantial effect on employment and on the employer (e.g., investment, production process, work location, product elimination). Type I decisions were part of the inherent freedom on the part of management to manage its affairs unrelated to employment, and there was no obligation on the part of the management to bargain over these decisions; type II decisions carried a bargaining obligation; and type III decisions were the difficult ones. Those were the ones in which the board would be required to determine whether the benefits from bargaining outweighed the costs the bargaining obligation placed on management in the conduct of its business (*First National Maintenance v. NLRB*). These decisions would also be the ones that would most likely directly affect competitiveness and employment protection/creation.

Like *Fibreboard*, *First National Maintenance* was a case involving a narrow set of facts wrapped in broad language. In *Fibreboard*, the Court found that the employer's decision to subcontract the work done by the unionized employees was based solely on labor costs, and found that the employer was obligated to bargain over the decision. On the other hand, in *First National Maintenance*, the Court found that the employer's decision to terminate its maintenance and cleaning contract with the nursing home had nothing to do with labor costs; therefore, the employer was not obligated to bargain with the union over the decision.

The question then became one of interpretation. Under what circumstances would the benefits to collective bargaining outweigh the burdens placed on the conduct of business so that bargaining would be required? Did the circumstances of a particular case bring it closer to *Fibreboard*, with its bargaining requirement, or to *First National Maintenance*, with no bargaining requirement? Ten years after *First National Maintenance*, the NLRB answered this question in *Dubuque Packing Company*, 303 NLRB No. 66, 1991 (enfd. 143 LRRM 301 [DC Cir., 1993]). In this case, the employer, a meatpacking firm, moved its hog kill operation from a location in Iowa to a location in Illinois. The question in the case was whether the employer had an obligation to bargain over this change. The Court distinguished between an employer decision that resulted in a basic change in the nature of the business, and one that did not result in such a change. The former decision would not trigger a bargaining obligation, but the latter would.

The Court decided that the employer decision in Dubuque was not a basic change in the nature of the business because it was a decision to relocate existing work rather than a change in the nature of the work the firm was doing. It was a decision regarding *where* the firm should be in a business (in this case, hog killing), not whether it *should* be in a business. It was not new work that the firm was undertaking, nor was the work being done in a new and different way. Moreover, the Court found that labor costs were a factor in the decision to move; therefore, bargaining could possibly have influenced the company's decision to relocate the work.

The foregoing discussion indicates that changes in capital structure or product mix of the firm that were made for the purpose of increasing firm competitiveness were generally not considered to be negotiable items with the union, even if such changes resulted in employment reductions. In such circumstances, the law permitted a decoupling of employer concerns with competitiveness and union concerns with job protection and creation. The law regarding the obligation to bargain permits employers who so choose to avoid discussions with a union representing their employees by stating that the decisions are type I decisions or type III decisions, which are basic changes in the nature of the business. Disagreements are resolved before the NLRB, resulting in litigation rather than negotiation.

The result of all this is that the law in the United States does not encourage companies and unions to negotiate over matters relating to competitiveness and job protection/creation. The focus of the law is not on problem solving or on linking the issues of competitiveness and job security. Rather, the focus is on the individual employer decision and whether or not the employer has the right to make that decision without negotiating with the union about it. Bargaining over competitiveness and employment protection/creation does occur, but not because the law encourages it—it occurs because both parties want it to, or because the employer believes that it cannot make a sufficiently strong case before the NLRB and the courts to avoid bargaining with the union.

The Political Environment

There is little government involvement in the bargaining process, which is indicated by the language quoted earlier from the insurance agents case. The Taft-Hartley Act (1947) has created the Federal Mediation and Conciliation Service (FMCS), and most states have created comparable agencies. Among the missions of the FMCS and the state agencies is the encouragement of labor and management to resolve their disputes. In addition, the FMCS provides training and other expert support for parties that wish to move toward a cooperative relationship (Block, Beck, and Kruger 1996). There is also a legal requirement in the NLRA that the FMCS and the state agency be notified if there is a labor dispute that has not resulted in an agreement. Although the FMCS and/or the state agency may contact the parties and offer their services, there is no legal requirement that the parties avail themselves of these services; they are completely voluntary. Indeed, if only one party declines to use the services, then the FMCS/state agency has no role.

This minimalist government involvement in bargaining in the United States may be contrasted with the situation in Canada, its largest trading partner. While Canadian provinces have extensive requirements for governmental mediation and conciliation before a work stoppage may be commenced, the United States has no requirements (outside railroads and airlines) for prestrike or prelockout governmental intervention in the absence of a national emergency. Thus, there is no requirement for a neutral, ameliorative influence in negotiations that may encourage otherwise recalcitrant parties to consider jointly addressing competitiveness and employment protection/creation (Block 1997).

The Institutional Environment

Just as there is no centralized corporatist structure in the United States to encourage the use of the collective bargaining systems for competitiveness and employment protection and creation, there is nothing in the institutional environment that encourages such a result. The two major actors, employers and unions, operate within decentralized internal systems. Each of the actors addresses its own internal interests in collective bargaining. The result is additional impetus for decentralization and variation in collective bargaining outcomes.

Employer Institutions

In the United States, there are no overarching employer institutions that can implement or encourage on a broad-based scale the use of collective bargaining for encouraging competitiveness and employment protection/creation. Consistent with the principle of decentralized collective bargaining, and in contrast to some other industrialized countries (Sisson 1987; Pellegrini 1998; Furstenberg 1998; Hammerstrom and Nilsson 1998), employers in the United States generally do not form coalitions or work collectively to bargain with unions at all, much less to encourage the use of the collective bargaining system as a vehicle for competitiveness and employment protection/creation. The structure of the system is that each employer makes a decision on the matter that it believes is in its best interest.[3] Employers in the United States are competitive firms first and employers second. They often use their labor relations systems as a vehicle for competitive advantage vis-à-vis other firms. Thus, if they believe that collective bargaining can be used to enhance competitiveness, they will so use it. On the other hand, if employers believe that collective bargaining makes it more difficult than otherwise to be competitive, they will resist collective bargaining.

Similarly, there is no employer institution that encourages the use of collective bargaining for employment protection.

The employer institutions that do exist, such as the Labor Policy Association, are primarily political lobbying organizations that disseminate information to the public and policymakers and support a point of view on labor and employment policy issues. The Labor Policy Association describes itself as "the nation's leading public policy association of senior human resource executives, representing more than 250 major corporations doing business in the United States." Among the items on its agenda is "to encourage legislative and regulatory bodies to improve labor and employment policies in order to enhance the competitiveness of companies doing business in the United States and enable employee friendly workplace practices" (Labor Policy Association 2001). Other organizations aim to keep labor relations and human resources management practitioners up to date. The Employment Policy Foundation, for example, is a "research and education foundation that promotes sound employment policy." It is supported by over 130 leading companies. Similarly, the Society for Human Resource Management is an information and educational organization.

Union Structures

Just as there is decentralization among employers, there is also decentralization among unions. The American Federation of Labor (AFL), established in 1881 as Federation of Unions, was established on the principle of international union autonomy in collective bargaining (Brooks 1971). Although the Congress of Industrial Organizations (CIO), established in 1938, was generally more centralized than the rival AFL, it too left collective bargaining to the affiliate organizations (Bernstein 1969). This principle was maintained when the two organizations merged in 1955 to form the AFL-CIO, and it continues in existence today. Thus, just as there is no centralized system or structure to encourage employers to move toward, there is no structure to encourage unions to consider the use of collective bargaining for competitiveness.

The level of the national (or international)[4] union in the United States represents a mixture of union structures and centralization and decentralization. The structural characteristic common to almost all unions in the United States is a local union chartered by the national union. Thus, at first blush, one might think that the local union is under the control of the national union, which could be a force for encouraging locals to use collective bargaining as a vehicle for competitiveness.

On the other hand, it is also true that there is wide variation in the nature of the relationship between local unions and the parent national, and the amount of autonomy the local has in collective bargaining. In general, when the negotiations of one local of a national union appear to affect the interests of another local of a national union, the national union will attempt to exert some control over the local collective bargaining activities. In addition, most national unions retain the right in their constitutions to approve collective agreements negotiated by their local unions. This provides the national with some ultimate control over the outcomes of bargaining (Fiorito, Gramm, and Hendricks 1991).

Thus, locals that negotiate for only one employer may have an interest in negotiating for increased competitiveness for that employer. Such impetus, however, must come from the local itself. The national union is not likely to encourage it. Whether the national union discourages it depends on whether the national perceives that a contract places other locals at a disadvantage.

Where multiple locals of the same union negotiate with the same employer, the national union will normally create a structure to develop common bargaining proposals. Such a structure can facilitate the use of collective bargaining to the extent the locals have an interest in doing so. Such a structure usually results in a multiplant, multilocal agreement covering wages, hours, and terms and conditions of employment. It may also create structures that encourage competitiveness, such as in the GM–UAW national agreement. Similarly, in the Alcoa case, we see the national union agreeing with corporate leadership on a partnership agreement.

Such bargaining structures must be implemented at the plant and local level. This may be done through a separate plant agreement, as in the GM–UAW case, or by administration of the master agreement, as in the Alcoa–Steelworkers case. The major concern of the international is that the local does not gain work at the expense of the other locals by a reduction of standards. In the absence of such a concern, the national union will generally provide the locals with autonomy.

Joint and Governmental Structures

There is only one formal overarching joint or governmental structure that encourages the parties to use collective bargaining to encourage competitiveness and employment protection/creation. The Collective Bargaining Forum was established in 1984 by a group of corporate chief executive officers and presidents of international unions under the auspices of the United States Department of Labor. Its purpose was to "address the role of collective bargaining in helping the United States maintain a rising standard of living in an increasingly competitive world economy" (Collective Bargaining Forum 1988). In April 1999, the forum issued a report entitled *Principles for New Employment Relationships*, which continued the theme of the importance of collective bargaining and mutual respect between employers and unions. Among the principles to which the report urged adherence were:

> acceptance in practice by union leaders and members of their responsibility to work with management to improve the economic performance of their enterprises in ways that serve the interests of workers, consumers, shareholders, and society and acceptance by corporations of employment security, the continuity of employment for its workforce, as a major policy objective that will figure as importantly in the planning process as product development, marketing, and capital requirements. (Collective Bargaining Forum 1999)

This report was announced by the vice president of the United States at a White House ceremony. It is noteworthy, however, that the president of the National Association of Manufacturers (NAM), a member of the forum, did not sign the report (Collective Bargaining Forum 1999).

This discussion indicates the extent of decentralization in the U.S. industrial relations system, both among the actors and between the actors and government (Collective Bargaining Forum 1999). That the NAM president chose not to sign the report, although his management colleagues were willing to do so, suggests that while executives of individual firms were willing to sign, the representative of a broad cross-section of industry was unwilling to agree to such principles on behalf of his constituency. This was the case even with the prestige of a vice-presidential announcement. Again, this reinforces the principle that such overarching structures can do nothing more in the United States than publicize the view that companies and unions should use the collective bargaining process to enhance competitiveness and employment protection/creation.

The Economic Environment

Economic policy in the United States over the last 20 years has generally taken a laissez-faire approach to employment and competitiveness. There has been little direct intervention in the marketplace to affect either of these. Rather, U.S. economic policy has been based on the principle that markets should be permitted to work, and that firms in general should be unconstrained in their options to allocate resources to their most productive uses, with a corresponding maximization of shareholder wealth.

Monetary policy has been based on limiting inflation, enhancing the operation of the market by reducing an important source of uncertainty. Concerns about job security have helped to restrain wage increases and, therefore, inflation (Board of Governors of the Federal Reserve System 1997).

Fiscal policy has been generally non-existent. For much of the last 20 years, taxes and government spending have been part of an ideological and political debate rather than an economic debate. This ideological/political debate is an aspect of a broader debate in the United States over the wisdom of government involvement in the economy.

Trade policy has advocated open markets and the reduction of barriers in the United States and among its trading partners (U.S. Trade Representative, Office of, 1999). It is true that the U.S. government will act, at times, to support domestic industries, such as the steel industry, that can persuade policymakers that it may be the victim of unfair trade practices by foreign competitors. Thus, the government has on occasion advocated for protection based on the position that an industry has been victimized by unfair trade practices (Lucentini 1999). But the general thrust of U.S. economic policy has been to open its markets and to expect other countries to do the same (U.S. Trade Representative, Office of, 1999).

The impact of such economic policies on collective bargaining in the United States can best be characterized as reinforcing the variation that exists in law and the decentralization that the actors have helped to create. The market approach of the U.S. economic policy has encouraged firms to respond to the economic environment by following strategies that are viewed as being in the best interests of the individual shareholders of the firm. These responses are individualistic and firm specific rather than coordinated among firms. The individual collective bargaining system of each firm has been forced to adjust to these firm strategies enabled by U.S. economic policies.

The foregoing discussion raises an obvious question: given the absence of systemic encouragement in the United States of the use of the collective bargaining system for competitiveness and employment protection, how frequently is the collective bargaining system used? While there have been case studies and anecdotal information regarding the relationship, they do not address the more general question of incidence.

Despite the absence of a broad-based data set on the incidence of innovations, there has been work that attempted to estimate the frequency of such innovations. Summarizing studies published in the 1980s Voos and Eaton (1992) observed that the evidence suggested that up to 65 percent of unionized firms in the surveys examined had created some form of innovation that could be considered to have a competitiveness-based rationale. The most frequent innovations were information sharing and employee surveys, at over 60 percent of the surveyed unionized firms. Fifty-one percent of the firms and unions in one survey had created quality circles, 29–46 percent had instituted some profit sharing, and 40 percent had established at least one participatory program. Reanalyzing data from a survey done by the U.S. General Accounting Office, Voos and Eaton determined that some form of participation was occurring in 79 percent of the unionized firms. Gain sharing was the least frequent innovation, occurring in 33 percent of the surveyed firms.

A different view of the frequency of use of collective bargaining as a vehicle for encouraging competitiveness and employment protection/ creation can be obtained by examining a volume published by the Industrial Relations Research Association (Voos 1994). This book examined collective bargaining in the 1980s and early 1990s in many of the unionized industries in the United States that have been affected by global competition and domestic market deregulation. Among the industries examined were paper, meatpacking, aerospace, steel, auto assembly, auto parts, trucking, telecommunications, and textile. A summary of the findings of these industry studies will provide some rough sense of the frequency of the use of collective bargaining as a vehicle for competitiveness and employment protection/creation. In a sense, the findings of this study would represent a lower bound on the incidence of the use of collective bargaining, because its researchers focused primarily on the large unionized firms and because the studies were not designed to examine the phenomenon. Thus, absence of a discussion of the use of collective bargaining for purposes of competitiveness and employment protection/creation does not necessarily mean that it was not so used in that industry. It is possible that the researcher simply did not address it. Nevertheless, the studies in this volume provide useful data.

Table 2.1 presents a summary of the results of the studies in the volume. The left-hand column displays the processes by which the outcomes were obtained, the outcomes in the form of shop floor changes, and the contexts/environments in which these outcomes occurred. An outcome was considered to have occurred if it appeared in one of the major firms in the industry.

The great diversity in U.S. collective bargaining has been documented elsewhere (Block, Beck, and Kruger 1996), and this diversity is evident in analyzing the incidence of the use of collective bargaining as a vehicle for addressing issues of competitiveness and job protection/creation. In some industries, the collective bargaining system has been used a great deal to address these problems; in others, less so. Paper, steel, aerospace, auto assembly, and telecommunications have all used the collective bargaining system as a vehicle for increasing firm competitiveness in at least one of the firms in the industry. This has been less the case for auto parts, motor carrier transportation, meatpacking, and textiles.

Competitiveness

With respect to competitiveness, the table suggests that auto assembly and steel are ahead of the other industries as sectors in which at least one of the major firms and unions is using the collective bargaining system as a tool to increase competitiveness. Auto assembly

Table 2.1 Incidence/Frequency of the Use of Collective Bargaining as a Means of Encouraging Firm Competitiveness and Employment Protection/Creation in the United States, 1980–1992

	Paper	Meat-packing	Aero-space	Steel	Auto assembly	Auto parts	Motor carrier	Telecom-munication	Textiles
Hard bargaining/conflict	x	x							
Adversarial/arm's length			x						
Outcomes									
Concessions									
Lump sum bonuses			x						
Two-tier wage systems									
High-level participation				x					
Shop-floor changes									
Imposed after hard barg.									
Elim. weekend OT	x								
Production teams	x								
Participative prog.	x								
Flex. between prod. and maint.	x								
Greater subcontracting rights	x								
EE involvement	x								
Quality circles			x						
Long contracts	x								
Jointly agreed-upon competitiveness									
Elim. weekend OT						x			
Production teams					x				
Participative prog.								x	

	1	2	3	4	5	6
Flex. classifications						x
Greater subcontracting rights						x
EE involvement						x
QWL and training					x	
TQMS					x	
Consultation on tech. change		x			v	
Information sharing				x		
Company-financed training	x			x		
Profit sharing			x	x		
Work restructuring				x		
Joint LM comms at all levels				x		
Seat on board				x		
Guaranteed income stream			x			
Pay for knowledge			x			
EE involvement						
Long-term contracts		x	x			
EE assignments, vacation, etc.		x	x			
Product development						
Variable pay	x					
Manufacturing methods						
Employment protection/creation						
Employment guarantee			x	x		
Employment security	x		x	x		

(continued)

Table 2.1 (continued)

	Paper	Meat-packing	Aero-space	Steel	Auto assembly	Auto parts	Motor carrier	Telecom-munication	Textiles
Context/environment									
Regulatory									
Antitrust litigation	x								
Environment	x								
OSHA/safety regs.	x						x		
Import controls (joint pressure)				x					
Deregulation							x	x	
Divestiture							x	x	
Globalization									
Value of dollar affects exports	x								
Corporate structure									
Mergers and acquistions									
Debt	x								
Uniform TCE "downward"	x								
Decentralization							x		
Technology									
Computerization	x								
Market structure									
New Entrants		x				x			
Customers									

Deregulation	x
Government spending	x

SOURCE: Voos (1994).

has instituted production teams, flexible classifications, joint training, pay for knowledge, and extensive employee involvement. The steel industry, primarily National Steel, has formal information sharing, company-financed training, profit sharing, work restructuring, and joint labor–management committees at all levels. In both of these cases, such changes were jointly agreed upon rather than being forced on the union by hard employer bargaining. The telecommunications industry has instituted company-financed training and variable pay. Similarly, aerospace has instituted consultation on technological change, total quality management systems, and quality of work life systems with training.

The paper industry has also used collective bargaining as a vehicle for increasing firm competitiveness. A major difference between the paper industry and the auto assembly, steel, telecommunications, and aerospace industries was the process by which the changes in the traditional collective bargaining system were implemented. In paper, the changes were made after hard bargaining by employers, and followed de-unionization campaigns by some paper companies in the late 1970s and early 1980s.

On the other hand, there was no substantial use of collective bargaining as a vehicle to increase in competitiveness in the meatpacking, auto parts, and motor carrier industries. All of these industries were characterized by strong de-unionization movements or substantial non-union sectors.

Recently, Gray, Myers, and Myers (1999) examined the U.S. Bureau of Labor Statistics file of collective agreements covering 1,000 workers or more that expired between September 1, 1997, and September 30, 2007. Of the 1,041 agreements in the study, 154 (or 14.8 percent) covering 854,803 workers contained contract provisions requiring high-performance work practices, generally designed to increase productivity and quality, reduce costs, increase the focus on the customer, and ultimately, improve the firm's competitiveness. These include continuous improvement and employee involvement programs, team concept, job security thorough training and multiskilling, creation of an oversight committee, and no layoffs due to the implementation of new work practices.

Two recent studies provide insight into whether unionization affects the frequency of innovative work practices. Based on a study using a sample of 664 establishments in 1992 from the Dun and Brad-street establishment file, Osterman (1994) found that roughly two-thirds of the establishments in which 50 percent of the core workers (defined as those workers who are actually involved in making the product produced by, or delivering the service provided by, the estab-lishment) participate had at least one of four identified practices (teams, job rotation, total quality management, and quality circles). There was no evidence that collective bargaining was related to the use of such programs. Gittleman, Horrigan, and Joyce (1998) also found no union effect on the incidence of work practices. Their estimates, based on a data set from the U.S. Department of Labor, found that 42 percent of all establishments, but about 70 percent of establishments with 50 or more employees, had one of six practices.[5]

Employment Protection/Creation

The U.S. collective bargaining system has not been able to generate widespread employment guarantees. Rather, employment security and job protection is obtained through the success of the firm. Put differ-ently, there is very little administered job protection or job security developed through the U.S. collective bargaining system. In general, job security is market-based. This phenomenon is illustrated in Table 2.1.

The results presented by Gray, Myers, and Myers (1999) support the assertion that administered job security is rare in the United States. Of the agreements covering 1,000 workers or more, only 22 of the agreements (2.1 percent) covering 123,811 workers had explicit provi-sions prohibiting layoffs, and only 14 agreements (1.3 percent) cover-ing 32,537 workers had no subcontracting provisions.

The most well-developed job security system in the United States is in the automobile assembly industry in the 1996 agreement between General Motors (GM) and the United Auto Workers (UAW) Union, in which both parties negotiated a system of secured employment levels (SELs). According to the agreement, the SEL system prohibits layoffs for any reason except market-related volume reductions, reasons beyond the control of the corporation ("acts of God"), sale of part of the corporation, model change or plant rearrangement, or layoff of an employee recalled to a temporary vacancy. National Steel and the

United Steelworkers of America, as part of their cooperative partnership, have negotiated job security over the life of the collective agreement (Arthur and Smith 1994).

Conclusion on Incidence

The results of this analysis indicate that while there has been much
written about new work practices and the use of collective bargaining
as a means for improving firm competitiveness in the United States,
multiple provisions encouraging or requiring the parties to create special structures for competitiveness are found only in a minority of
major collective agreements. There continues to be a bias in the U.S.
collective bargaining system toward retaining the formalism in the traditional, adversarial U.S. model of collective bargaining. As unionization does not appear to be related to the frequency of such practices, it
suggests that the preference of the parties to collective bargaining for
the traditional model is comparable to the extent of the preference to
maintain the traditional hierarchical system of work organization.

This does not mean that unions and employers are not working
toward competitiveness. As the case studies demonstrate, such efforts
are often ad hoc and not incorporated into agreements. Indeed, parties
often prefer to avoid placing such programs in the collective agreement
because placing them in the agreement reduces the flexibility of either
party to pull out if it wishes. In essence, placing the cooperative process within the requirements of the legally enforceable collective
agreement is inconsistent with the essential voluntariness of cooperation. Nevertheless, these results suggest that formal collective bargaining provisions addressing competitiveness and employment protection/
creation efforts are not as common as might be thought based on the
literature.

SUMMARY AND CONCLUSIONS

There are no societal institutions in the United States that encourage unions and employers to use the collective bargaining system for
purposes of firm competitiveness and employee job security. While the

law enables collective bargaining to be used for this purpose, the law does not require it. In addition, the decentralized structure of unionization permits employers to explore competitiveness options away from the union. Legal ambiguity about whether firm investment decisions are negotiable, along with associated litigation, reduces the likelihood that collective bargaining will be used to address competitiveness and job security.

Government in the United States generally has little involvement in collective bargaining, as bargaining is seen as a matter for the parties. Nongovernmental aggregating institutions for management are lobbying, advocacy, or educational organizations, and do not encourage collective bargaining as a vehicle for addressing competitive and job security. On the union side, although union structures may have the potential for encouraging use of bargaining for competitiveness and job security, decentralized bargaining makes it difficult for high-level union structures to impose outcome preferences on lower-level structures.

The result of this is great variability in the extent to which firms and industries use collective bargaining to address issues of firm competitiveness and job security. Some firms and industries have actively used their bargaining systems to pursue competitiveness; others have not. Job security is rarely provided explicitly; rather, it is linked to competitiveness.

Notes

The author thanks Ms. Betty Barrett for her research assistance.

1. Whether public policy in the United States succeeds in protecting that choice is a matter of debate. See, for example, U.S. Departments of Commerce and Labor (1994) and Block, Beck, and Kruger (1996).
2. Employees of private, for-profit health care institutions had been previously covered through the board's normal exercise of jurisdiction.
3. A notable exception to this rule is in over-the-road trucking and automobile hauling. See Belzer (1994).
4. The highest union level in the United States often designates itself an international union, perhaps because it may have membership in Canada.
5. See Appelbaum and Batt (1994) for a review of survey evidence on the incidence of new work systems in the United States without taking into account unionization. Appelbaum and Batt indicate that up to 85 percent of the firms in the United

States had at least one practice in one facility, but the percentage dropped to as low as 25 percent on multiple practices.

References

Appelbaum, Eileen, and Rosemary Batt. 1994. *The New American Workplace: Transforming Work Systems in the United States*. Ithaca, New York: ILR Press.

Arthur, Jeffrey, and Suzanne Konzelmann Smith. 1994. "The Transformation of Industrial Relations in the American Steel Industry." In *Contemporary Collective Bargaining in the Private Sector*, Paula B. Voos, ed. Madison, Wisconsin: Industrial Relations Research Association, pp. 135–180.

Belzer, Michael. 1994. "The Motor Carrier Industry: Truckers and Teamsters under Siege." In *Contemporary Collective Bargaining in the Private Sector*, Paula B. Voos, ed. Madison, Wisconsin: Industrial Relations Research Association, pp. 259–302.

Bernstein, Irving. 1969. *Turbulent Years: A History of the American Worker*. Boston, Massachusetts: Houghton-Mifflin, pp. 1933–1941.

Block, Richard N. 1995. "Labor Law, Economics, and Industrial Democracy: A Reconciliation." *Industrial Relations* 34(3): 402–416.

———. 1997. "Rethinking the National Labor Relations Act and Zero-Sum Labor Law: An Industrial Relations View." *Berkeley Journal of Employment and Labor Law* 18(1): 30–55.

Block, Richard N., John Beck, and Daniel H. Kruger. 1996. *Labor Law, Industrial Relations, and Employee Choice: The State of the Workplace in the 1990s*. Kalamazoo, Michigan: W.E. Upjohn Institute for Employment Research.

Board of Governors of the Federal Reserve System. 1997. 85th *Annual Report*. Washington, DC: Government Printing Office, Washington, DC

Brooks, Thomas R. 1971. *Toil and Trouble*. 2d ed. New York: Dell.

Collective Bargaining Forum. 1988. "New Directions for Labor and Management: Views from the Collective Bargaining Forum." U.S. Department of Labor, Bureau of Labor Management Relations, BLMR 120.

Collective Bargaining Forum. 1999. "Principles for New Employment Relationships." In *BNA Daily Labor Report* 83(April 30): E-1–E-6.

Detroit Newspaper Agency. 1998. 325 NLRB 64.

Evening News Association. 1965. 164 NLRB 1494, enfd. 372 F.2d 569 (6th Cir., 1967).

Fiorito, Jack, Cynthia L. Gramm, and Wallace E. Hendricks. 1991. "Union Structural Choices." In *The State of the Unions*, George Strauss, Daniel G. Gallagher, and Jack Fiorito, eds. Madison, Wisconsin: Industrial Relations Research Association, pp. 103–138.

Furstenberg, Friedrich. 1998. "Employment Relations in Germany." In *International and Comparative Employment Relations*, 3d ed., Greg. J. Bamber and Russell Lansbury, eds. London; Thousand Oaks, California; New Delhi: Sage Publications, pp. 201–223.

Gittleman, Maury, Michael Horrigan, and Mary Joyce. 1998. "Flexible Workplace Practices: Evidence from a Nationally Representative Survey." *Industrial and Labor Relations Review* 52(1): 116–135.

Gray, George, Donald W. Myers, and Phyllis Myers. 1999. "Cooperative Provisions in Labor Agreements: A New Paradigm." *Monthly Labor Review* 122(1): 29–45.

Hammerstrom, Olle, and Tommy Nilsson. 1998. "Employment Relations in Sweden." In *International and Comparative Employment Relations*, 3d ed., Greg. J. Bamber and Russell Lansbury, eds. London; Thousand Oaks, California; New Delhi: Sage Publications, pp. 224–248.

Keyserling, Leon. 1945. "Why the Wagner Act?" In *The Wagner Act after Ten Years,* Louis B. Silverbert, ed. Washington, DC: Bureau of National Affairs.

Labor Policy Association. 2001. "LPA Connect." Available at www.lpa.org.

Lucentini, Jack. 1999. "ITC Reverses Anti-Dumping Duties for Steel Imports." *Journal of Commerce,* May 12, p. 11.

Millis, Harry A., and Emily Clark Brown. 1950. "The Wagner Act to Taft-Hartley: A Study of National Labor Policy and Labor Relations." Chicago, Illinois: University of Chicago Press.

Osterman, Paul. 1994. "How Common is Workplace Transformation and Who Adopts It?" In *Industrial and Labor Relations Review* 47(2): 173–188.

Pellegrini, Claudio. 1998. "Employment Relations in Italy." In *International and Comparative Employment Relations*, 3d ed., Greg. J. Bamber and Russell Lansbury, eds. London; Thousand Oaks, California; New Delhi: Sage Publications, pp. 144–168.

Sisson, Keith. 1987. "*The Management of Collective Bargaining: An International Comparison.*" Oxford and New York: Basil Blackwell.

U.S. Departments of Commerce and Labor. 1994. *Commission on the Future of Worker Management Relations, Report and Recommendations*. December, Washington, DC.

U.S. Trade Representative, Office of. 1999. *USTR Releases 1999 Inventory of Trade Barriers*. News Release 99-30, April 1.

Voos, Paula, ed. 1994. *Contemporary Collective Bargaining in the Private Sector.* Madison, Wisconsin: Industrial Relations Research Association.

Voos, Paula, and Adrienne Eaton. 1992. "Unions and Contemporary Innovations in Work Organization, Compensation, and Employee Participation." In *Unions and Economic Competitiveness*, Lawrence Mishel and Paula Voos, eds. Armonk, New York, and London: M.E. Sharpe, pp. 173–215.

3
The Impact of Collective Bargaining on Competitiveness and Employment

A Review of the Literature

Dale Belman
Richard N. Block
Michigan State University

How does collective bargaining affect the performance of the firm? Does it improve or worsen productivity? Does collective bargaining inherently increase costs? Are organized firms less profitable than those which are not organized? Does union organization lower stockholder returns and discourage new investment? Are organized firms more likely to fail than non-union firms? These questions have been a topic of research, and of controversy, for more than a century. For most of this period, researchers have sought to answer these questions through detailed institutional analyses of firms and industries with *Union Policies and Industrial Management* (Slichter 1941), which provides a landmark example. In the last 20 years, econometric methods have been brought to bear on these questions. Beginning with "Trade Unions in the Production Process" (Brown and Medoff 1978), more than 60 published articles have examined some aspect of the collective bargaining/firm performance relationship in the United States. The literature has grown sufficiently large—and remained controversial—that there are four extant reviews: Hirsch and Addison (1986), Addison and Hirsch (1989), Belman (1992), and Kuhn (1998).

GENERAL THEORETICAL CONSIDERATIONS

Standard static economic models provide little room for unions to have a positive effect on firm performance. In the static model, firms in competitive industries operate on their efficiency frontiers. Unions, interlopers in an already efficient production process, affect firms by increasing compensation and negotiating rules that reduce the flexibility of work practices. Both lead to higher production costs and lower profits. Higher wages and benefits of organized firms increase costs and reduce profits, although these effects may be partially counteracted if firms use their escalated compensation to attract more productive employees. The labor productivity of organized firms may also be higher than that of unorganized firms if they adjust to escalated labor costs by substituting capital for more expensive labor. Despite such adaptations, organized firms are seen as experiencing higher production costs and reduced profits, because they have been moved away from the profit-maximizing combination of inputs. The effects of higher compensation are magnified where unions negotiate work rules that limit management flexibility. Such rules move firms inside their efficiency frontier, further degrading firm performance. The lower profits and consequent lower rates of return on investment realized by organized firms lead to lower levels of investment and increase the likelihood of firms' failure.

An implicit assumption of these models, one required for firms to operate on their efficiency frontier, is that employee effort is fully under the control of the firm and therefore maximized (Altman 2000). While this reasonably holds where managers and owners have complete information on their employees' actions and can impose sanctions in the absence of maximum efforts, in situations in which the marginal transaction costs of writing effort-specific labor contracts, metering and monitoring employees, and enforcing the contracts exceed their marginal benefits (which is likely to be the case in the vast majority of firms), employees will be afforded some discretion over their work efforts. It is probable that firms can monitor and control the physical effort expended by employees. Employee discretion over effort is likely to be greatest, however, and most difficult for firms to monitor when that effort involves sharing employee-specific information with the firm that can be used to enhance firm performance. Firms which, because of the nature of their employment relationship, fail to elicit the full discretionary information-sharing effort of their employees will suffer some degree of x-inefficiency and operate inside their efficiency frontier. The lesser technical efficiency of such firms may, however, be balanced by reduced direct labor costs if their "employment package" is less generous than that of firms which better elicit employee effort and have higher output per unit of labor input. Where employees have some control over work effort, different approaches to the employment relationship may successfully coexist and be equally effective at minimizing costs.

If a firm is operating below its efficiency frontier, there may be conditions under which unions would enhance firm performance. Building on Altman's approach, unionization may be viewed as a reorganization of the production process, providing advantages and disadvantages for the firm. On the one hand, unions may have all the negative efficiency effects contemplated by the leaner, traditional economic theories. On the other hand, the representative and protective functions of unions may provide opportunities for firms to better their performance by eliciting greater commitment and information-sharing effort from their employees than would be forthcoming in the absence of a union. Employee information sharing is likely to be greater in a unionized than in a non-union setting for two reasons: 1) collective bargaining mandates negotiation and contact between the employer and elected employee representatives, thus providing established channels that are accepted by employees; and 2) employees can negotiate over the "price" to be paid for this information, perhaps in the form of increased compensation, or guarantees that they will not be disadvantaged. In regimes lacking employee representation, the rules of the workplace are often uncertain and their interpretation is, in the final analysis, made unilaterally by an interested party. Under such conditions, employees are likely to try to secure and improve their position through opportunistic behavior such as reserving knowledge that is potentially useful to the firm. Such behavior is less necessary where there is employee representation, as there are established interpretations of rules and a structure that provides substantive and procedural due process.[1] Thus, unions and collective bargaining may improve firm performance by providing employee collective voice to which employers are legally required to listen.

In a non-union setting, with no formal, legally mandated voice mechanism, employees' fundamental means of communicating dissatisfaction with the employment relationship is through exit. This is costly, as the firm loses trained and productive employees. In contrast, unions provide a protected forum through which employees can make their views known to their employer and reduce the impetus for employees to leave the firm. The representative function of the union also provides a structure through which the employer can elicit a frank response to contemplated changes in the employment relationship and seek employees' untrammeled consent. Collective voice is particularly important where the labor force has divergent interests, and where changes in production arrangements and employment policies will have divergent effects on the labor force. Collective organization provides a means through which employees can negotiate among themselves and develop a mutually acceptable arrangement with the employer.

Unionization may also improve firm performance by forcing improvements in managerial performance. The costs of poor management may be mitigated in a non-union workplace as bad production planning, and inconsistent labor policies may be offset by low pay and exceptional flexibility in the deployment of labor. Such solutions are more expensive—if not unavailable—under collective bargaining, where inordinate and ill-considered use of overtime, sudden shifts in employment, and inconsistencies in the application of rules are limited by the agreement. In order to survive and profit, organized firms have to improve their planning of production and the quality of their supervision, in essence being "shocked" into efficient production practices.

Unions may also solve problems related to information, transaction costs, and public goods through the hiring and training of employees. In industries such as construction, where the term of employment with any individual employer is short and there is substantial occupational skill and knowledge, firms will be reluctant to undertake training as they are unlikely to recover their costs. Unions potentially provide a structure under which employers can collectively finance training programs for employees who will, over their working lives, be shared among those firms. The union may also play an oversight role, ensuring that employers adhere to the training regime required to provide appropriately skilled employees. In labor markets where employees are transient among firms, unions may also serve to certify the skills of employees and reduce the time and expenditure required to locate appropriately skilled employees.

A similar public goods situation might also exist outside construction. The longer employer tenure of unionized employees increases the return from firm-specific training, as unionized employees are less likely than their non-union counterparts to quit and take their training elsewhere (see Freeman and Medoff 1986).

A final suggestion of the literature is that industrial relations climate rather than union organization, per se, is the key variable in determining the effect of collective bargaining on organizational performance. Collective organization can provide a mechanism through which managers and employees propose, discuss, and agree upon the organization of the firm. In such circumstances, the firm is likely to be more efficient than one in which decisions are taken unilaterally by management. In contrast, where relations between managers and employees are conflictual, collective organization becomes a tool in that conflict. It may be that the nature of the employment relationship, the level of trust between the parties, the history of unilateralism or mutuality, and the parties' acceptance of the legitimacy of one another's goals play key roles in determining the effectiveness of an organization, whether unionized or non-union, as well as the effectiveness of collective bargaining on organizational performance.

The foregoing theoretical discussion points out that the efficiency effects may not be as straightforward as traditional, lean economic theories would predict. While collective bargaining and unionization may negatively affect firms' efficiency on the production frontier, it is not likely that very many firms operate on that frontier at all times. Once the assumption of efficient production in the absence of a union is relaxed, it is possible to conceive of situations in which the presence of a union might enhance efficiency, or be associated with no effect. Thus, the predicted effects of unions on firm performance are not unambiguously negative. The matter is best determined by empirical work, and it is to that work that this chapter now turns.

EMPIRICAL RESEARCH ON COLLECTIVE BARGAINING AND ORGANIZATIONAL PERFORMANCE

Empirical research on the effect of collective bargaining on organizational performance typically addresses one of four broad topics: 1) the effect on firm productivity and costs; 2) the effect on productivity growth; 3) the effect on firm profits, investment, and survival; and 4) the role of industrial relations climate on organizational outcomes. Drawing on Belman (1992) and on Kuhn (1998), we review the literature on the United States up to the early 1990s and supplement this with a discussion of more recent research.[2]

Effects on Productivity and Costs

The effect of unions on firm productivity and costs has been studied by comparisons across industries, within industries, and within firms. While the former has the advantage of providing more general answers to the question of interest, the more narrowly defined within-industry and within-firm studies are advantageous in using measurement of inputs and outputs and models that better reflect the industry or organization under study. For example, while inter-industry studies must use price-based measures of output, such as value added, industry studies may use physical as well as price-based measures of output.

There are only two inter-industry studies of productivity and costs: Brown and Medoff (1978) and Clark (1984). The former, which considers the effect of union density on state by industry-value added, suggests that organized establishments are between 19.5 and 24 percent more productive, depending on the controls incorporated into the model. Using a product line data set for 250 large firms, Clark finds a small, economically inconsequential union effect on productivity. Belman (1992) suggests that the difference between these findings might be reconciled if positive productivity effects are the consequence of shock effects in less well managed small and mid-sized firms. Larger firms, such as those found in Clark's sample, may already be well managed and so do not benefit from organization. Neither study indicates that unions have a consistently negative effect on productivity, as suggested by standard theory.

Intra-industry studies of the effect of unions on productivity and costs are more prevalent than inter-industry studies. These include the cement industry (Clark 1980a,b), construction (Allen 1984, 1986a,b, 1988b; Cavalluzzo and Baldwin 1993), hospitals (Sloan and Adamache 1984; Register 1988), banking (Graddy and Hall 1985), coal (Connerton, Freeman, and Medoff 1983; Boal 1990; Boal and Pencavel 1994; Byrnes et al. 1987), wooden furniture (Frantz 1976), machining (Kelley and Xue 1990), steel finishing (Ichniowski and Shaw 1995), and trucking (Delery et al. 2000). Considering the studies prior to 1992, Belman (1992) concluded that the effects of unions on productivity and costs vary by industry and by the period under consideration. There is scant evidence that unions act to reduce productivity. The only consistent negative finding was in the banking sector, while there is substantial evidence that unions act to improve productivity in many industries. Clark's work on cement plants finds that organization is associated with a productivity shock effect of 7 to 12 percent. The extensive work on construction by Allen suggests that organization is associated with higher productivity, particularly on projects that require higher-skilled workers.

Union effects on costs are less clear-cut than union effects on productivity. Unions reduce unit costs in private construction but are associated with higher unit costs in public construction. Later work by Cavalluzzo and Baldwin (1993) suggests that labor productivity was 38 percent higher on organized construction sites. The outcomes in construction are of particular interest because of the role that building trades unions play in the training process and in reducing employer search costs.

Extractive industries have a reputation for conflictual labor relations, and studies of bituminous coal confirm the centrality of industrial conflict in determining unions' effect on productivity (Kerr, Harbison, and Dunlop 1960). Byrnes et al. (1987) found that organized surface mines were more productive than their non-union counterparts. Connerton, Freeman, and Medoff (1983) found that the effect of unions on mine productivity varied: in periods of labor peace, organized mines were 30 percent more productive than non-union mines; in periods of industrial conflict, organized mines were 15 percent less productive than non-union mines. Boal (1990) considers the effect of unions on productivity in the 1920s, while Boal and Pencavel (1994) examine the effect on days of operation from 1897 to 1937. The first finds that unions did not affect productivity in larger mines in the 1920s but were associated with lower productivity in smaller mines. Boal suggests that this is the result of the lesser sophistication in labor relations in smaller mines. Boal and Pencavel find no relationship between unionization and days of operation except for the period from 1921 to 1930, when mines in fully organized counties had 25 percent fewer operating days than mines in unorganized counties. Although the authors suggest that this is the result of unions' limitation of days of work, this was also a period of intense conflict—conflict that eventually led to federal military intervention, as the industry in West Virginia de-unionized. The negative effect of organization on operating days is then as likely to have reflected the events around the long strike, such as the Matewan Massacre and the Battle of Beal Mountain as a commitment to limiting working days.[3]

Bronars, Deere, and Tracy (1994) and Hirsch (1991b) are unique in using Compustat data to examine the effect of unions on multiple measures of firm performance, including profitability, investment, sales, employment growth, and productivity.[4] Bronars, Deere, and Tracy use the union contract files of the Bureau of Labor Statistics to obtain matching data on the extent of organization by firm. The authors test several specifications and compare results obtained with their firm level unionization measure with the use of more aggregate measures of union density. Although results vary considerably by specifications, the findings suggest that firms with higher unionization have higher productivity in manufacturing, suggesting that unionized employers offset the union wage and benefit premium through improved productivity. Outside manufacturing, the relationship is too sensitive to specification, functional form, and period to support any conclusions about union effects.[5] This research considers whether unions influence other aspects of firm performance, including capital expenditures, capital-to-labor ratios, advertising-to-sales ratios, and investment in research and development, and it finds little evidence for any effect.

In contrast, Hirsch (1991b) finds that organized firms are substantially less productive than similar non-union firms. Data on unionization were obtained from a survey of Compustat firms. Initial estimates indicate that firms with the average level of organization (42.3 percent) would have 3.5 percent lower factor productivity as measured by value added per employee. The results are sensitive to inclusion of industry controls. Models with no controls for industry indicate much larger negative union productivity effects; estimates from models that include highly disaggregate measures of industry find union productivity effects in the range of −1 to −1.5 percent. Conflation of industry effects with firm unionization is also apparent in the preferred estimate, which incorporates measures of the characteristics of two-digit industry, including a measure of industry union density. The coefficient on industry density is positive and sufficiently large in magnitude: a 10-percentage-point increase in industry density would be associated with a 2.8-percentage-point increase in firm productivity, to potentially off-set the negative effect of firm union density. Hirsch speculates that this effect is due to escalated product prices in heavily organized industries or incomplete specification of the determinants of productivity corre-lated with industry density. The sensitivity of the estimates to industry controls may, however, reflect measurement problems in the construc-tion of the dependent variable, value added per employee, suggesting that the estimates of union effects may be inaccurate.[6]

Two recent studies provide indirect evidence of a negative union productivity effect in steel and in trucking. Ichniowski and Shaw's 1995 study of steel finishing lines focuses on the determinants and con-sequences of human resource management practices. They find that human resource management (HRM) practices cluster on a continuum from traditional to new and that the cluster of the newest practices is associated with a 6 percent higher ratio of actual to scheduled operat-ing time. Organized plants, however, are substantially less likely to adopt new HRM practices. Although the authors do not test the effect of unions on operating time per se, by reducing the likelihood that firms adopt more efficient HRM practices, unions are potentially asso-ciated with lower productivity. Delery et al. (2000) examine the premise that organized firms have lower turnover and quit rates among trucking firms with 30 or more employees. Their evidence suggests that, after accounting for the effect of unions on wages, neither unions nor "voice" procedures are associated with reduced turnover or quits.[7]

Taken together, current studies remain favorable to the view that collective bargaining typically has a favorable positive effect on the productivity performance of the firm, suggesting that non-union firms rarely operate at maximum efficiency. The union effects, however, vary considerably by industry and by time period, and they are sensitive to the degree of conflict between employees and employers. Where it has been studied, the effect of unions on costs is typically less favorable as gains in productivity are offset by escalated compensation costs.

Effects on Profitability, Investment, and Firm Failure

While studies of productivity and costs are fundamentally about the effect of collective bargaining on firm efficiency, studies of profitability consider both the efficiency and distributional effects of bargaining. Although any negative effect on profits may originate in reduced efficiency, it may also result from unions using bargaining power to claim part of the profits typically going to shareholders. Research interest has focused on the subsidiary issue of the circumstances under which unions can claim a share of firm profits. In competitive markets, unions' claim of a share of capital income would result, in time, in the firm going out of business as new capital was diverted from reinvestment in the company. Once the assumption of competitive markets is relaxed, however, the long-run results of union diversion of profits to compensation become difficult to predict. For example, where a firm realizes rents from market power in imperfectly competitive markets, the firm may generate sufficient profits to maintain investment at an optimal level. In such a situation, the union compensation premium may be a diversion from other uses of profits, such as dividends. In addition, unions may be able to claim quasi-rents from physical investment where such investment is not readily reversed and is long lived.

Studies of profitability, the most common topic of research, may be divided between those that use firm data to construct measures such as price/cost margins ([sales − payroll − materials costs] / sales) and Tobin's q (value of firms equity and debt / replacement cost of assets), and those that use stock market data to assess the effect of changes in union status and collective bargaining outcomes on the valuation of firm stocks. An almost universal result from these studies is that unions are associated with reduced profitability. What remains at issue is circumstances under which unions are able to claim a share of firm profits.

Freeman (1983), Freeman and Medoff (1984), Karier (1985, 1988), and Voos and Mishel (1986) have estimated the effect of unions on profitability using industry data obtained from the U.S. Census. Although such studies suffer the disadvantage of using data averaged across firms within an industry, the data reflect firms' domestic (U.S.) operations, simplifying the specification of equations and providing an appropriate match between dependent and explanatory variables. Freeman and Freeman and Medoff find that price/cost margins are reduced between 0 and 37 percent and return on capital was reduced between 9 and 32 percent in the presence of unions, but that unions did not reduce firms' profitability in competitive markets. Karier finds similar results with unions reducing price/cost margins by 14 percent in highly monopolized markets but having no effect in competitive markets. Voos and Mishel find that unions reduce price/cost margins by between 22 and 35 percent but do not consider the effect of competitiveness of the market.

Studies of firms are potentially superior to industry studies, because the lower level of aggregation may allow researchers to better isolate the mechanisms through which unions affect profitability. This advantage is purchased at the cost of challenges in collection of data. Data on the firm unionization are not available from standard sources; researchers must locate appropriate sources and compile the data. Becker and Olson (1992) used pension data collected by the U.S. Department of Labor to estimate union density for large firms; Hirsch (1991a) conducted a survey of Compustat firms that collected data on organization; Bronars, Deere, and Tracy (1994) use data from the Bureau of Labor Statistics collective bargaining agreement file to determine unionization levels within the firm. All of these approaches result in partial samples of the population of firms. Hirsch reports obtaining data from 620 of 1,900 Compustat firms initially surveyed, and Bronars et al. sample sizes range from 120 to 130, less than 10 percent of the Compustat firms. Such extensive incomplete coverage raises the potential for substantial nonrandomness in the sample and consequent bias in the estimates.[8] A second daunting problem is that because measures of firm profitability include profits from overseas operations, the models need to incorporate controls for the extent and performance of overseas operations. The absence of controls for foreign operations from any of the firm estimates shadows this literature.[9]

Finally, Standard & Poor's Compustat data are limited to very large firms and, as such, are unrepresentative of the economy as a whole.

Belman (1992) reviews studies by Salinger (1984), Clark (1984), Hirsch and Connolly (1987), Connolly, Hirsch, and Hirschy (1986), Becker and Olson (1992), Voos and Mishel (1986), and Allen (1988a,b). As with the industry studies, these studies suggest that organized firms have lower price/cost margins and lower q's than firms that are not organized. For example, Clark found that unions reduced returns on sales by 16 percent while reducing returns on capital by 19 percent. As in the industry studies, another issue is whether unions reduce the profits of all firms, or only of firms that are earning economic rents. Salinger's work suggests that unions reduce monopoly rents. Hirsch and Connolly (1987), however, do not support this conclusion. They find that unions capture rents from sunk research and development investments. These results are specific to Tobin's q but are not found when price/cost margins are the dependent variable.[10] Becker and Olson (1992) also find that the negative relationship between unionization and profits is related to union capture of rents on intangibles, but, as with Hirsch's research, these results are sensitive to the measure of profit. In contrast to other studies, Allen finds that unions do not reduce profits in construction. The unique nature of unionism in construction, which results in substantial employer savings in recruitment and training costs in a transient labor market for generally skilled employees, may account for this difference.

More recent research is provided by Hirsch (1990, 1991a,b, 1992), Hirsch and Morgan (1994), and Bronars, Deere, and Tracy (1994). Hirsch's extensive work on this issue builds on his survey of firms in the Compustat database to determine the company's extent of unionization in the 1970s and 1980s.[11] These data were then matched to Compustat panels on firms to measure the relationship between firm unionization and various measures of firm performance between 1972 and 1980. Depending on the specification used, Tobin's q is 20 percent lower, and return on capital, π, is 14 percent lower in the typical union firm (with union density of 42.3 percent). Estimates of the effect of unions on profits are, however, sensitive to controls for industry, particularly to inclusion of industry indicator variables. In the presence of such indicators, the coefficient on firm density becomes nonsignificant for q and becomes small and only marginally significant for π.[12] Further estimates suggest that the reduced profitability of organized firms may be attributed to unions appropriating rents from firms' investments in research and development and fixed capital and that, as a result, organized firms may invest less than unorganized firms in research and development and fixed capital.[13] These results are consistent with unions capturing rents where firms are unable to protect those rents from partial appropriation through collective bargaining. Building on prior work by Becker and Olson (1986), Hirsch and Morgan (1994) find that shareholder risks decline with the extent of union coverage in the 1970s. They found that highly unionized firms had lower returns during this period but that this relationship between shareholder returns and coverage broke down in the 1980s.

Bronars, Deere, and Tracy (1994) also examine the effect of unionization on profitability for three measures of profitability: Tobin's q, the ratio of excess market valuation to sales, and the ratio of net operating income to sales, using several specifications. Focusing on the specifications that include controls for industry and firm characteristics, there is no evidence that Tobin's q or the ratio of excess valuation to sales is lower among organized firms in the manufacturing sector, but the net operating income to sales ratio in fully organized firms is estimated to be 3 to 4 percent below that of an otherwise similar non-union firm. Among the nonmanufacturing firms, Tobin's q in a completely organized firm would be 18 to 22 percent below that of a similar unorganized firm, but there is no significant union effect on the other measures of profitability. First, differencing of the data eliminates any meaningful statistical relationship between unionization and profitability except for a negative effect for the ratio of excess market valuation to sales in nonmanufacturing. The sensitivity of the estimates to the sector, measure of profitability, and specification of the variables suggests that although some specifications of the profits equation produce the expected negative relationship, that relationship is tenuous, particularly in the manufacturing sector.[14]

Stock market studies consider the effect of events related to collective bargaining on the market value of firms. Under the assumption that stock markets are efficient processors of information, changes in stock valuation in response to new information reflect the expected effect of these shifts on the performance of the firm. Changes in stock valuation

in response to strikes, representation elections, and settlement of contracts will then reflect unions' effect on firm outcomes.

Events that are viewed as favorable to unions are generally associated with a reduction in the market valuation of the firm's stock.
Rubeck and Zimmerman (1984) find a decline in stock valuation both
when a petition for a representation election is filed and when the election is held. Stock valuation declines between 1.3 percent if the union
loses and 3.8 percent if it wins. Both Greer, Martin, and Reusser (1980)
and Becker and Olson (1986) found a decline in stock valuation following a strike. In contrast, concessionary contracts were associated
with an increase in stock valuation (Becker 1987). Although these
results might indicate that stockholders expect organized firms would
operate less efficiently, it may also reflect a belief that union success
will lead to the redistribution of profits from stockholders to employees. There is also internal evidence in these studies that profit declines
preceded organization and that union activity might be a response to
worsening economic performance.

Freeman and Kleiner (1999) consider the effect of organization on
the survival of firms. In the first part of this study, the authors use
Compustat data to examine the likelihood of a firm going out of business. Using a modest set of controls, the authors find that organization
itself reduces the likelihood of a firm becoming insolvent but that the
likelihood of insolvency rises with the level of organization. The most
highly organized firms have a 23 percent likelihood of becoming insolvent, relative to a 19 percent probability of insolvency for non-union
firms, for the period under consideration. In the second part of the
study, the displaced worker supplement of the Current Population Survey is used to determine the effect of union membership on the probability that an employee was displaced by the permanent closure of a
plant. Freeman and Kleiner's estimates indicate that union membership
is unrelated to plant closing or any form of displacement. They suggest
that these results are consistent with the hypothesis that unions behave
in an economically rational manner in not increasing wages to the point
at which the firm, plant, or business lines close down.

Taken together, the studies of the effect of collective bargaining on
profits, investment, and firm failure suggest that unions do not fully
pay for their higher wages and benefits through increasing productivity
and reducing costs. They act to redistribute part of the shareholders'

earnings to employees, but this redistribution occurs where firms are earning rents or quasi-rents. However, the redistribution is not so large as to endanger the economic viability of the firm.

Collective Bargaining Practices and Competitiveness

The previous discussion focused on the effect of the mere incidence of collective bargaining on organizational outcomes that might be associated with the competitiveness of the firm. There is no reason to believe, however, that the existence of a bargaining relationship per se would necessarily result in improved firm competitiveness. Collective bargaining traditionalists might contend that the major purpose of collective bargaining is to provide employees with workplace representation rather than to encourage firm competitiveness. To the extent that this is the case, only when the union and the employer believe it is in their mutual interests to move the process toward encouraging competitiveness will it be used that way.

Since the early 1980s, many firms and unions have moved toward innovative collective bargaining and cooperative relationships as a means for fostering improved firm competitiveness and increased employment protection and job creation (Kochan, Katz, and McKersie 1986; Block, Beck, and Kruger 1996). A literature has developed that has examined the success of these innovations, and much of the pre-1990s literature is included in Belman's 1992 review. A series of studies of General Motors (Katz, Kochan, and Gobielle 1983; Kochan, Katz, and Mower 1985; Katz, Kochan, and Weber 1985) investigated the relationship between innovative industrial relations programs, industrial relations outcomes, and plant-level economic performance. They suggest that such programs have positive effects on the quality of production and a weaker but positive effect on labor efficiency (productivity). These studies also find that higher levels of conflict, such as escalated levels of grievance filing and disciplinary activity, are associated with reduced product quality and productivity. Schuster (1983) examined the impact of profit-sharing plans, gain-sharing plans, labor–management committees, quality circles, and quality of work life program on productivity (sales per employee hour worked), employment, product quality, absenteeism, voluntary turnover, tardiness, grievances, and employment security with a before-and-after study of 38 firms in the eastern United States. Such programs had a positive impact on productivity but little effect on product quality, employment, turnover, absenteeism, tardiness, and the grievance rate. There was a strong linkage between employment security guarantees and firms' economic performance, but only 3 of 38 firms provided such guarantees.

Rubinstein (2000) examined the difference in first-time product quality associated with union and non-union at the comanaged Saturn plant in Tennessee. Rubinstein found that the communications networks associated with union managers were associated with higher first-time quality than the communications networks associated with non-union managers.

Several studies suggest that the availability of formal procedures for resolving grievances is associated with improved firm performance but that escalated levels of grievance activity are associated with lower productivity and product quality (Norsworthy and Zabala 1985; Ichniowski and Lewin 1987; Ichniowski 1986; Goldberg and Brett 1979; Spencer 1986). Ichniowski finds that the absence of a mechanism for resolving grievances in a non-union paper mill resulted in the firm operating 19.5 percent below full labor efficiency.

Although the relationship between the quality of the collective bargaining relationship and firm performance has not been widely studied in the 1990s, there have been several notable additions to the literature. In a survey based on 194 plant mangers, 74 union officers, and 135 headquarters personnel associated with the same firms, Cooke (1990) found that high union leader involvement and frequent team meetings were associated with perceived improvements ("much improvement") in quality, productivity, and supervisor–employee relations. Measures of technological displacement had a mixed effect on these outcomes, while concession bargaining measures were unrelated. In a study of 194 manufacturing firms throughout the United States and 131 manufacturing firms in Michigan, Cooke (1992) found that unionized firms with jointly administered employee participation programs achieved greater improvement on a subjective measure of product quality than unionized firms without such programs, and that unionized firms with jointly administered programs achieve quality gains equal to non-union firms with participation programs. Subcontracting was found to have a negative spillover on quality: firms that used subcontracting suffered reduced product quality relative to firms that did not subcontract. Summarizing these findings, Cooke suggests that labor–management climate was a key determinant of quality.

In a study of the economic impact of the change in the collective bargaining relationship between Xerox and the Amalgamated Clothing and Textile Workers, Cutcher-Gershenfeld (1991) finds that work areas that could be identified as traditional (adversarial) were associated with significantly higher product costs, greater losses to scrap, greater productivity variation, and lower net return (a measure of actual vs. standard labor hours for producing a part) than work areas identified as transformational or transitional (work areas that exhibited less measured conflict, greater speed of conflict resolution, problem solving, worker autonomy, and worker-initiated changes).

Kelley and Harrison (1992) report that the presence of labor–management committees in a sample of small unionized machining plants was associated with lower levels of productivity and greater job insecurity. They suggest that this unexpectedly negative relationship is the result of omitted mediating variables, such as vulnerability to foreign competition. In their view, the adoption of labor–management committees is not random but a response to poor economic performance by the firm. The presence of these committees may proxy for omitted variables that are the true source poor performance.

The current literature provides considerable favorable evidence on the effect of innovative work structures on organizational performance. Evidence on the role of unions in promoting or impeding the implementation of new work practices is mixed. Ichniowski and Shaw (1995) find that organized steel finishing lines are less likely to adopt the most advanced combination of work practices. Osterman (1994) finds more mixed results in a study of the adoption of innovative work practices, where such practices are defined by the adoption of teams, job rotation, quality circles, and total quality management. The effect of unions on innovation depends greatly on the construction of the independent variable, with the estimated effect varying from positive and weakly significant to nonsignificant to negative and weakly significant. Eaton and Voos (1992) suggest that the unions play an important role in obtaining the genuine consent and participation of the labor force, and that this makes adoption of workplace innovations both more likely and effective. They suggest that, with the exception of profit-sharing plans, organized plants are more likely to adopt work-place innovations than non-union plants.

Evidence on the effect of unions on training is mixed. Unions appear to have little effect on the amount of training in small firms, but they are associated with longer duration and total hours of training and a greater use of formal training programs in a more representative cross-section of firms. In a study of the effect of government subsidies on firm training, Holzer et al. (1993) found that the presence of a union did not affect the amount of annual quality-related training hours offered by a population of small manufacturing firms in the years 1987–1989; training hours were determined primarily by whether the firm received a government subsidy. In addition, there was no evidence suggesting that the presence of a union affected the success of that training, measured by a change in the scrap rate. Using a 1992 survey of the Small Business Administration, Black, Noel, and Wang (1999) find that weekly hours of formal and informal training are not affected by the union status of firms. Organized firms, however, provide more weeks of on- and off-site formal training than otherwise comparable firms. A larger fraction of the training provided by organized firms is formal, while non-union firms provide a larger fraction of their training as informal training by managers or co-workers.

Summarizing the knowledge as of the early 1990s, Belman (1992) wrote:

> There is substantial variation in the effect of unions on firm per-formance and this variation is caused by differences in the rela-tionship between labor and management. Low trust/high conflict environments, rather than unions, are the source of reduced pro-ductivity. Higher levels of trust are associated with reduced strife and, consequently, with both greater productivity and higher prod-uct quality. Further, although the level of conflict is affected by the conditions and history of a plant, firm and industry, the parties can reduce the level of conflict and share the gains from improved efficiency and quality. (Pp. 69–70)

Current evidence supports the view that special efforts by labor and management to address issues of competitiveness improve product quality and productivity but their effects may not be large. Rarely is labor relations the basis on which the firm maintains its position in the product (Block et al. 1987). Thus, labor relations is a contributor to firm competitiveness, but it is not reasonable to expect labor relations to be the leading determinant of corporate performance.

Collective Bargaining and Employment

Standard static neoclassical economic theory predicts that collective bargaining is associated with lower levels of employment, although more developed theories suggest different possibilities. In the standard theory, collective bargaining imposes labor costs on employers above what they would otherwise incur. Assuming competitive product and labor markets and operation on its production frontier, a firm will respond to above-market labor costs associated with collective bargaining by substituting capital for labor, thereby reducing employment. If the firm is unable to substitute capital for labor, it would operate below the level of maximum efficiency, with lower employment than otherwise due to forgone revenues.

Contract curve or efficient contract theory suggests a somewhat different result, as the union does not simply set a monopoly wage. Rather, the union bargains with the firm for a wage that is between the competitive and monopoly wage and a level of employment that is above the monopoly and potentially above the competitive employment level. In such instances, collective bargaining might be associated with higher rather than lower employment.

The negative employment effects contemplated by the standard static model may also not be found if collective bargaining improves productivity. In this case, the effects of the escalated wages are substantially and possibly fully offset by the productivity improvements associated with collective bargaining. As organized firms' unit labor costs are no higher than that of non-union firms, employment will not decline. If the productivity gains from organization are of sufficient magnitude, organized firms may have lower unit labor costs and higher employment than their non-union counterparts. This form of productivity gain is distinct from that which results when firms respond to escalated union wages by substituting capital for labor. While increasing the capital stock will boost labor productivity, it will, other things equal, be associated with a decline in employment. If union labor is itself more productive independent of the complementary capital stock, the increase in productivity occurs without any increase in capital stock or decline in employment.

The interpretation of any negative employment findings is complicated by a U.S. legal system that allows firms to escape collective bargaining by investing away from the union. Under the U.S. system, a firm may decide to eschew the difficult and expensive strategy of directly eliminating collective bargaining in a plant that is already organized. An alternative strategy is to accept collective bargaining where it exists but strongly resist organization in new plants and focus new investment in new, non-union plants. Employment declines in the union sector as the capital stock that complements the unionized employees becomes depreciated and obsolete. Thus, a negative relationship between unionization and employment growth might then be the result of capital-stock-obsolescence-driven employment attrition in unionized plants and union avoidance rather than direct adjustments to escalated wages or other economic responses to collective bargaining.

A limitation of all of these models is that they make predictions about the level of employment but say little about how collective bargaining affects the rate of growth of employment. Some authors, such as Leonard (1992), suggest that the reduced rates of profit predicted by the standard neoclassical model will cause organized firms to have a lower rate of employment growth, but these arguments are intuitive and not derived from a formal model.

As noted by Kuhn (1998), research on the effect of unions on employment in the United States is sparse.[15] Leonard (1992) investigates this issue with a sample of 1,798 California manufacturing plants over the period between 1974 and 1980. In a model that included controls for initial employment, corporate structure, percentage of nonclerical white-collar workers in the plant labor force, and industry and regional indicators, employment in unionized plants grew 9 percent more slowly than employment in non-union plants. When the sample was separated by the union status of the plant, average annual employment growth rates were 4 percent lower in unionized plants. When information on the vintage of plants was incorporated into a subsample for which such information was available, there was no statistically significant difference in the growth rates of union and non-union plants. The latter result suggests that the slower growth of employment in organized plants may be due to unions' inability to organize newer facilities rather than any effect on employment growth rates per se.

As part of their study of Compustat firms, Bronars, Deere, and Tracy (1994) found that the employment growth was significantly slower among organized firms than among non-union firms. Employment in non-union manufacturing grew between 0.5 and 1.0 percentage points faster than among organized firms, and between 0.6 and 1.1 percentage points faster among firms outside manufacturing.

Employment effects may also reflect union preferences. In a study of bargaining behavior of locals of the International Typographical Union in 13 small towns, MaCurdy and Pencavel (1986) found that locals did not maximize rents at the expense of employment in negotiations with newspapers. Rather, consistent with the efficient contracts model, they accepted lower wages to minimize employment loss. In contrast, in a study of employment in two-digit industry manufacturing industries in 1972 and 83 construction projects in 1973–1974, Wessels (1991) found a consistently negative relationship between unionization and employment. Although significance varied by specification, the results suggested that the relationship between collective bargaining and employment was better described by a standard neoclassical model. The difference in the results between the MaCurdy and Pencavel and Wessels studies may reflect differences between the industries under study, as well as the varied goals and concerns of labor organizations. The lower employment levels found on organized construction projects is also consistent with the substantially greater productivity of unionized workers found by Allen (1984, 1988a).

Dunne and MacPherson (1994) find that there was little correlation between unionization rates by industry and plant closing between 1977 and 1982. However, industries with higher rates of organization had a higher rate of employment loss due to contractions of plants and somewhat smaller job gains associated with plant expansions. Consistent with the standard neoclassical theory, Linneman, Wachter, and Carter (1990) find that the decline in employment in unionized industries is greatest in those industries with the largest union/non-union wage differentials.

SUMMARY AND CONCLUSIONS

Although standard economic theory generates straightforward pre-dictions regarding the effect of unions and collective bargaining on organizational performance, other more complex theoretical formula-tions suggest that the effects of unions may be ambiguous and difficult to predict *a priori*. The empirical research supports the latter position, and suggests that unions and collective bargaining often have a posi-tive rather than negative effect on productivity. As unions generally increase costs of production, these results suggest that management is generally able to adjust its production processes and employment lev-els to unionization. Unions are also associated with lower profitability than their non-union counterparts. Whether this negative effect on profitability has a long-term negative impact on firm viability is deter-mined by whether this union appropriation of profits is from dividends or from internally financed investment and research and development. Effects of unions and collective bargaining on other measures of orga-nizational performance, such as product quality and training, tend to be negligible (or positive) but small, suggesting that collective bargaining does not alter these outcomes relative to what they would otherwise have been in the absence of unions. There is evidence that cooperative and nontraditional collective bargaining structures have a positive impact on workplace outcomes, such as productivity and quality, but have little effect on overall organizational performance. Finally, there is some evidence of a negative employment effect associated with col-lective bargaining and unionization, although it is difficult to determine whether such effects are the result of union workplace practices or employer opposition to unionism.

Overall, the effects of unions and collective bargaining are as var-ied as might be expected in an economy with decentralized bargaining structures and organizations with differing production functions, often operating at less than maximum efficiency and participating in markets with varying degrees of competitiveness. Straightforward predictions about the effects of unions on firm performance are likely to be an extreme oversimplifacation.

Notes

1. Although it is possible for non-union employers to create voluntary employee voice structures without union representation, in order to remain lawful, such structures may not incorporate bilateral communications over terms and conditions of employment. In addition, because these structures are controlled by the employer, and because the employees lack protection, employees may be less likely to share knowledge for fear it may be used to their disadvantage.
2. There has been no new literature on the effect of unions on productivity growth since Belman's review, and we omit this issue from our review.
3. This interpretation is reenforced by the Boal and Pencavel finding that unions raised wages by a meager 5 percent in this period. It is unlikely that an organization that had the ability to reduce operating days by one-quarter would settle for such a small wage advantage that the members' income was lower than their non-union counterparts.
4. Discussion of issues involved in the use of firm data is put off to the section on the effect of unions on firm profits.
5. Results range from negative and significant for 1975–1978 data with a Cobb-Douglas with industry and additional controls, to positive and significant for 1979–1982 data with a Cobb-Douglas with industry and additional controls, to negative and significant for the same year and specification when estimated with a frontier approach.
6. Hirsch (1991b) reports that labor costs, an essential element in the calculation of value added, are only available for one-quarter of the firms in the sample. For the balance of the sample, labor costs are constructed by assigning industry average labor costs to firms and assigning a 25 percent premium in labor costs to organized firms. This will create the observed negative correlation between unionization and value added as well as a strong correlation between industry and value added, and suggests that the estimates of firm level union productivity effects may be the result of construction rather than an underlying relationship. These problems are unfortunate, as the conventional measure of productivity—output per unit of labor—could have been constructed from Compustat data.
7. Delery et al.'s (2000) research is hampered by the low response rate to his survey and the even lower response to questions on turnover and quit rates.
8. Hirsch (1991b) reports that the means for his sample are similar to the means for the Compustat for the period under study. A more complete approach would have been to test the means and variances to ensure that data came from similar distributions and, because of the importance of industry to the study, to test means and variances by industry.
9. The omission of controls for foreign operations is the consequence of applying specifications developed for census industry/establishment data, which is limited to domestic operations, to data on firms which includes foreign operations.

10. Using a cross-section of New York firms, Hirsch and Link (1987) find that union-ization is associated with firm managers perceiving their firms as being less inno-vative than their competitors.

11. Hirsch's approach to obtaining firm-level unionization data differs from that of Becker and Olson (1992), who used pension data to determine firm unionization, and of Bronars, Deere, and Tracy (1994), who used the collective bargaining files at the Bureau of Labor Statistics to determine the extent of organization. The sur-vey was sent to 1,904 firms, and useable replies were obtained from 475 firms. This was supplemented with data from an additional 157 firms, which reported in a 1972 survey by the Conference Board. The final sample size was 632 firms.

12. The effect of controls for industry is found in Hirsch (1990). Similar results appear to characterize Table 4.4 of Hirsch (1991b) but, due to a misprint, this is not certain.

13. The measure of π is the gross return on capital (income plus depreciation plus interest income less inventory and imputed income adjustments) per unit of capi-tal. Firm profitability is more typically constructed as net income per unit of capi-tal, or as net operating income per unit of sales, and it is uncertain whether the results for π as constructed by Hirsch would obtain with the more conventional measures.

14. Although current studies treat unionization as a strictly exogenous variable, it may be simultaneous with profitability. One explanation of this is that unions seek to organize more profitable firms, resulting in a positive causal link between prof-itability and organization. A second possible explanation suggests that under U.S. labor law, large firms resist unionization by replacing union facilities with non-union facilities and resisting organization of non-union plants. Resisting unions is costly and is likely pursued more effectively by profitable firms and industries. This suggests a negative causal relationship from profitability to unionization. Either causal link would result in bias in estimates of the unionization/profitability relationship, which did not allow for simultaneity, but the direction of the bias is uncertain.

15. As in the balance of this review, we do not include articles that center on other countries or in which discussion and analysis of the United States is incidental. This reflects the focus of this review, and with regard to empirical work, authors view that cross-country measures of differences in employment relation systems are difficult to construct and their results even more difficult to interpret. Two articles that attempt to sort out the effects of international institutions on employ-ment growth are Addison, Teixeira, and Grosso (2000) and Buchele and Chris-tiansen (1999).

References

Addison, John T., and Barry T. Hirsch. 1989. "Union Effects on Productivity, Profits, and Growth: Has the Long Run Arrived?" *Journal of Labor Economics* 7(1): 72–105.

Addison, J.T., P. Teixeira, and J. Grosso. 2000. "The Effect of Dismissal Protection on Employment: More on a Vexed Theme." *Southern Economic Journal* 67(1): 105–122.

Allen, Steven G. 1984. "Unionized Construction Workers Are More Productive." *Quarterly Journal of Economics* (May): 251–274.

———. 1986a. "Unionization and Productivity in Office Building and School Construction." *Industrial and Labor Relations Review* (January): 212–242.

———. 1986b. "The Effect of Unionism on Productivity and Privately and Publicly Owned Hospitals and Nursing Homes." *Journal of Labor Research* (Winter): 59–68.

———. 1988a. "Productivity Levels & Productivity Change under Unionism." *Industrial Relations* 27(1): 94–113.

———. 1988b. "Human Resource Polices and Union–Non Union Productivity Differences." Working paper 2744, National Bureau of Economic Research, Cambridge, Massachusetts.

Altman, Morris. 2000. "Labor Rights and Labor Power and Welfare Maximization in a Market Economy." *International Journal of Social Economics* 27(12): 1252–1269.

Becker, Brian E. 1987. "Concession Bargaining: The Impact on Shareholders Equity." *Industrial and Labor Relations Review* (January): 268–279.

Becker, Brian E., and Craig Olson. 1986. "The Impact of Strikes on Shareholder Equity." *Industrial and Labor Relations Review* 39(3): 425–438.

———. 1992. "Unions and Firm Profits." *Industrial Relations* 31(3): 395–415.

Belman, Dale. 1992. "Unions, the Quality of Labor Relations, and Firm Performance." In *Unions and Economic Competitiveness*, L. Mishel and P.B. Voos, eds. New York: M.E. Sharpe, Inc., pp. 41–107.

Black, D.A., B. Noel, and Z. Wang. 1999. "On-the-Job Training, Establishment Size, and Firm Size: Evidence for Economics of Scale in the Production of Human Capital." *Southern Economic Journal* 66(1): 82–100.

Block, R., M. Kleiner, M. Roomkin, and S. Salsburg, eds. 1987. *Human Resources and the Performance of the Firm*. Wisconsin: Industrial Relations Research Association.

Block, Richard N., John Beck, and Daniel H. Kruger. 1996. *Labor Law, Industrial Relations and Employee Choice: The State of the Workplace in the 1990s.* Hearings of the Commission on the Future of Worker–Management Relations, 1993–94. Kalamazoo, Michigan: W.E. Upjohn Institute for Employment Research.

Boal, William M. 1990. "Unionism and Productivity in West Virginia Coal Mining." *Industrial and Labor Relations Review* 43(4): 390–405.

Boal, William M., and John Pencavel. 1994. "The Effect of Labor Unions on Employment, Wages, and Days of Operation: Coal Mining in West Virginia." *Quarterly Journal of Economics* 109(1): 267–298.

Bronars, Stephen, Donald Deere, and Joseph Tracy. 1994. "The Effects of Unions on Firm Behavior: An Empirical Analysis Using Firm-Level Data." *Industrial Relations* 33(4): 426–451.

Brown, Charles, and James Medoff. 1978. "Trade Unions in the Production Process." *Journal of Political Economy* 86(3): 355–378.

Buchele, R., and J. Christiansen. 1999. "Employment and Productivity Growth in Europe and North America: The Impact of Labor Market Institutions." *International Review of Applied Economics* 13(3): 313–332.

Byrnes, Patricia, Rolf Fare, Shawna Grosskopf, and C.A. Knox Lovell. 1987. "The Effect of Unions on Productivity: U.S. Surface Mining of Coal." Working paper 87-8, Department of Economics, University of North Carolina.

Cavalluzzo, Linda, and Dennis Baldwin. 1993. "Unionization and Productive Efficiency." In *The Measurement of Productive Efficiency: Techniques and Applications*, Harold O. Fried, C.A. Knox Lovell, and Shelton S. Schmidt, eds. New York, Oxford, Toronto, and Melbourne: Oxford University Press, pp. 210–220.

Clark, Kim B. 1980a. "The Impact of Unionization on Firm Productivity." *Industrial and Labor Relations Review* 33(4): 451–469.

———. 1980b. "Unionization and Productivity: Micro-Economic Evidence." *Quarterly Journal of Economics* 95(4): 613–639.

———. 1984. "Unionization and Firm Performance: The Impact of Profits, Growth, and Productivity." *American Economic Review* 74(5): 893–919.

Connerton, M., R.B. Freeman, and J.L. Medoff. 1983. "Industrial Relations and Productivity: A Study of the U.S. Bituminous Coal Industry." Photocopy, Harvard University, Cambridge, Massachusetts.

Connolly, R.A., B.T. Hirsch, and M. Hirschy. 1986. "Union Rent Seeking, Intangible Capital, and Market Value of the Firm." *Review of Economics and Statistics* 68(4): 567–577.

Cooke, William N. 1990. "Factors Influencing the Effect of Joint Union–Management Programs on Employee–Supervisor Relations." *Industrial and Labor Relations Review* 43: 587–603.

————. 1992. "Product Quality Improvement through Employee Participation: The Effects of Unionization and Joint Union–Management Administration." *Industrial and Labor Relations Review* 46(1): 119–134.

Cutcher-Gershenfeld, Joel. 1991. "The Impact on Economic Performance of a Transformation in Workplace Relations." *Industrial and Labor Relations Review* 44(2): 241–260.

Delery, John E., Nina Gupta, Jason D. Shaw, G. Douglas Jenkins Jr., and Magot L. Ganster. 2000. "Unionization, Compensation, and Voice Effects on Quits and Retention." *Industrial Relations* 39(4): 625–645.

Dunne, Timothy, and David E. McPherson. 1994. "Unionism and Gross Employment Flows." *Southern Economic Journal* 60(3): 727–738.

Eaton, Adrienne E., and Paula B. Voos. 1992. "Unions and Contemporary Innovations in Work Organization, Compensation, and Employee Participation." In *Unions and Economic Competitiveness,* L. Mishel and P.B. Voos, eds. New York: M.E. Sharpe, Inc., pp. 173–211.

Frantz, J. 1976. "The Impact of Unions on Productivity in the Wooden Household Furniture Industry." Undergraduate thesis, Harvard University, Cambridge, Massachusetts.

Freeman, Richard B. 1983. "Unionism, Price–Cost Margins, and the Return to Capital." Working paper number 1164, National Bureau of Economic Research, Cambridge, Massachusetts.

Freeman, Richard B., and Morris M. Kleiner. 1999. "Do Unions Make Enterprises Insolvent?" *Industrial and Labor Relations Review* 52(4): 510–527.

Freeman, Richard B., and James L. Medoff. 1984. *What Do Unions Do?* New York: Basic Books.

————. 1986. "The Two Faces of Unionism." In *Reading in Labor Economics and Labor Relations*, 4th ed. Lloyd G. Reynolds, Stanley H. Masters, and Colletta H. Moser, eds. Englewood Cliffs, New Jersey: Prentice-Hall, pp. 374–390.

Goldberg, Steven B., and Jeanne M. Brett. 1979. "Wildcat Strikes in Bituminous Coal Mining." *Industrial and Labor Relations Review* 32(4): 465–483.

Graddy, Duane B., and Gary Hall. 1985. "Unionization and Productivity in Commercial Banking." *Journal of Labor Research* 6(3): 249–262.

Greer, Charles W., Stanley A. Martin, and Ted A. Reusser. 1980. "The Effect of Strikes on Shareholder Returns." *Journal of Labor Research* 1(Fall): 217–231.

Hirsch, Barry T. 1990. "Market Structure, Union Rent Seeking, and Firm Profitability." *Economics Letters* 32: 75–79.

————. 1991a. "Union Coverage and Profitability among U.S. Firms." *The Review of Economics and Statistics* 73(1): 69–77.

—————. 1991b. *Labor Unions and the Economic Performance of Firms*. Kalamazoo, Michigan: W.E. Upjohn Institute for Employment Relations.

—————. 1992. "Firm Investment Behavior and Collective Bargaining Strategy." *Industrial Relations* 31(1): 95–121.

Hirsch, Barry T., and John T. Addison. 1986. *The Economic Analysis of Unions: New Approaches and Evidence*. Boston, Massachusetts: Allen and Unwin.

Hirsch, Barry, and R.A. Connolly. 1987. "Do Unions Capture Monopoly Profits?" *Industrial and Labor Relations Review* 41(1): 118–136.

Hirsch B.T., and A.N. Link. 1987. "Labor Union Effects on Innovative Activity." *Journal of Labor Research* 8(Fall): 3232–3332.

Hirsch, Barry T., and Barbara A. Morgan. 1994. "Shareholder Risk and Returns in Union and Nonunion Firms." *Industrial and Labor Relations Review* 47(2): 302–318.

Holzer, Harry J., Richard N. Block, Marcus Cheatum, and Jack H. Knott. 1993. "Are Training Subsidies Effective: The Michigan Experience." *Industrial and Labor Relations Review* 46(4): 625–636.

Ichniowski, Casey. 1986. "The Effects of Grievance Activity on Productivity." *Industrial and Labor Relations Review* 40(1): 75–89.

Ichniowski, Casey, and David Lewin. 1987. "Grievance Procedures and Firm Performance." In *Human Resources and the Performance of the Firm*, C. Olson and B. Becker, eds. Madison, Wisconsin: Industrial Relations Research Association.

Ichniowski, Casey, and Kathryn Shaw. 1995. "Old Dogs and New Tricks: Determinants of the Adoption of Productivity-Enhancing Work Practices." *Brookings Papers on Economic Activity: Microeconomics*. Washington, DC: Brookings Institute, pp. 1–55.

Karier, Thomas. 1985. "Unions and Monopoly Profits." *Review of Economics and Statistics* 62(1): 34–42.

—————. 1988. "New Evidence on the Effect of Unions and Imports on Monopoly Power." *Journal of Post Keynesian Economics* 10(3): 414–427.

Katz, Harry C., Thomas A. Kochan, and Kenneth R. Gobielle. 1983. "Industrial Relations Performance, Economic Performance, and QWL Programs: An Interplant Analysis." *Industrial and Labor Relations Review* 37(1): 3–17.

Katz, Harry C., Thomas A. Kochan, and Mark Weber. 1985. "Assessing the Efforts of Industrial Relations Systems and Efforts to Improve the Quality of Working Life on Organizational Effectiveness." *Academy of Management Journal* (September): 509–526.

Kelley, Maryellen R., and Bennett Harrison. 1992. "Unions, Technology and Labor–Management Cooperation." In *Unions and Economic Competitive-*

ness, L. Mishel and P.B. Voos, eds. New York: M.E. Sharpe, Inc., pp. 247–282.

Kelley, Maryellen R., and Lan Xue. 1990. "Does Decentralization of Programming Responsibilities Increase Efficiency? An Empirical Test." In *Ergonomics of Advanced Manufacturing and Hybrid Automated Systems, Volume II*, W. Karwoski and M. Rahini, eds. New York: Elsevier, pp. 105–137.

Kerr, Clark, Fredrick Harbison, and John T. Dunlop. 1960. *Industrialism and Industrial Man: The Problems of Labor and Management in Economic Growth*. Cambridge, Massachusetts: Harvard University Press.

Kochan, Thomas A., Harry Katz, and Robert McKersie. 1986. *The Transformation of American Industrial Relations*. New York: Basic Books.

Kochan, Thomas A., Harry C. Katz, and Nancy R. Mower. 1985. "Worker Participation and American Unions." In *Challenges and Choices Facing American Unions*, Thomas A. Kochan, ed. Cambridge, Massachusetts: MIT Press, pp. 271–314.

Kuhn, Peter. 1998. "Unions and the Economy: What We Know, What We Should Know." *Canadian Journal of Economics* 31(5): 1033–1056.

Leonard, Jonathan. 1992. "Unions and Employment Growth." *Industrial Relations* 31(1): 80–94.

Linneman, Peter D., Michael L. Wachter, and William H. Carter. 1990. "Evaluating the Evidence on Union Employment and Wages." *Industrial and Labor Relations Review* 44(1): 34–53.

MaCurdy, Thomas E., and John H. Pencavel. 1986. "Testing between Competing Models of Wage and Employment Determination in Unionized Markets." *Journal of Political Economy* 94(3): S3–S39.

Norsworthy, J.R., and Craig A. Zabala. 1985. "Worker Attitudes, Worker Behavior, and Productivity in the U.S. Automobile Industry, 1959–1976." *Industrial and Labor Relations Review* (July): 544–557.

Osterman, Paul. 1994. "How Common Is Workplace Transformation and Who Adopts It?" *Industrial and Labor Relations Review* 47(2): 173–188.

Register, Charles A. 1988. "Wages, Productivity, and Costs in Union and Nonunion Hospitals." *Journal of Labor Research* 9(4): 325–345.

Rubeck, Richard, and M.B. Zimmerman. 1984. "Unionization and Profitability: Evidence from the Stock Market." *Journal of Political Economy* 92(6): 1134–1157.

Rubinstein, Saul A. 2000. "The Impact of Co-Management on Quality Performance: The Case of the Saturn Corporation." *Industrial and Labor Relations Review* 53(2): 197–218.

Salinger, M.A. 1984. "Tobin's *q*, Unionization, and the Concentration–Profits Relationship." *Rand Journal of Economics* 15(2): 159–170.

Slichter, Sumner H. 1941. *Union Policies and Industrial Management.* Washington, DC: Brookings Institution.

Schuster, Michael. 1983. "The Impact of Union–Management Cooperation on Productivity and Employment." *Industrial and Labor Relations Review* 36(3): 415–430.

Sloan, Frank A., and Killard W. Adamache. 1984. "The Role of Unions in Hospital Cost Inflation." *Industrial and Labor Relations Review* (January): 252–262.

Spencer, Daniel. 1986. "Employee Voice and Employee Retention." *Management Journal* (September): 488–502.

Voos, Paula, and Lawrence Mishel. 1986. "The Union Impact on Profits in the Supermarket Industry." *Review of Economics and Statistics* 68(3): 513–517.

Wessels, Walter J. 1991. "Do Unions Contract for Added Employment?" *Industrial and Labor Relations Review* 45(1): 181–193.

4
Case Study Methodology

Richard N. Block
Michigan State University

This chapter will address the methodology used in the four case studies presented in the following chapters. As this was a study of the relationship among collective bargaining, employment protection/creation, and firm competitiveness, it was our initial view that the case study methodology should take into account all three major components to the extent possible. The review of the literature suggested, however, that formal, negotiated job protection was fairly rare in the collective bargaining system in the United States. Therefore, while we examined the extent of formal job security guarantees, we did not expect to find this a common occurrence.

In carrying out the case studies, we did not explicitly address the concepts discussed in Chapter 1, i.e., individualism, property rights, and transaction or value-based employment, as these concepts are embedded in the very nature of employment. Rather, our interest was in seeing how these concepts were manifested in the relationship as the parties attempted to address the goals of competitiveness and job security. Individualism is not seen in these case studies, because these are employment relationships that are collectivized. But property rights and transaction or value-based employment are the essence of these case studies, as will be discussed.

FRAMEWORK

The importance of property rights in the United States results in a highly decentralized system of collective bargaining. Public policy permits firms and unions, with firms generally being the more influential party because of property rights and their control of resources (Block 1990), to determine the type of collective bargaining system they wish. Bargaining outcomes, defined as wages, hours, working conditions, and the processes through which employers and unions interact, are determined at the level of the bargaining relationship.[1]

Because of decentralization of bargaining in the United States, we chose to focus the study at the plant or site level. Consistent with an industrial relations system approach (Dunlop 1958), we examined the parties' collective bargaining response to job protection/creation and competitiveness as the outcome to be examined. Because these were plant-level case studies, we focused on the two contextual constraints that would be most relevant at the plant level: the technological characteristics of the workplace and the market constraints, both key determinants of employment in a system of value-based jobs. Government, both as an actor in the system and as creator of constraints, plays a secondary but not unimportant role. At the plant level, the impact of government is felt not as a component of the locus of power in society or as an actor in the system, but as part of the competitive environment through policies that affect how business is conducted.

Using the Kochan, Katz, and McKersie (1986) framework, the focus of this study is at the workplace tier—the lowest-level tier—of the three-tier system. It may be expected, however, that there will be occasional interaction between the workplace tier and the two higher-level tiers, the strategic policy tier at the top and the collective bargaining/human resources policy tier in the middle. It is likely that bargaining structure matters; therefore, interactions between the workplace level and the two higher levels would be expected to be greater in a relationship that is part of a multisite bargaining unit than a relationship that is a single-site bargaining unit.

The most salient feature of the U.S. industrial relations system is the structured, written, legally enforceable, fixed duration collective bargaining contract. Crucial to this research was an examination of the traditional view that the collective agreement was the key component of the collective bargaining system in these facilities. A widely held view is that the collective bargaining agreement contract, with its inherent inflexibility, is a substantial impediment to firm competitiveness because it fails to adjust the employment bargain to market changes in a timely manner. If parties believed that these agreements served a useful purpose but at the same time were an impediment to desired flexibility, then flexibility could be obtained in the presence of a formal agreement by informal, extracontractual, unwritten, and legally unenforceable arrangements.

If many of the important innovations occurred outside the collective bargaining agreement, it would suggest that the U.S. collective bargaining system is far more flexible than might otherwise be recognized. It would also suggest that the focus on the collective agreement as the major characteristic of the collective bargaining system would be too narrow an approach to understand the true nature of the collective bargaining system, at least at these sites.

Thus, a key component of this study was to determine whether the parties established extracontractual structures for competitiveness and job protection, and if so, to describe them. If these structures existed, we also asked why they were created and whether competitive pressures may have had an effect on the nature of these structures.

METHODOLOGY

As noted, the basic methodology was the case study. The three key components of a case study are the selection of the sites to be studied, the nature of the data collected at the site, and the data collection procedure. Each of these will be examined.

The Sites

Site selection was based on the nature of the research needs, constrained by access. With respect to the nature of the research, we attempted to obtain sites that represented a range of businesses/industries, product types/production processes, and competitive environments to permit us to make reasonably generalized inferences. While we also hoped to attain some geographic variability within the sample, given globalization of the markets for many products produced in the unionized sector, this factor was given only secondary importance in site selection.

Access, of course, was essential. Inquiries were initiated based on the above criteria through contacts developed through the School of Labor and Industrial Relations at Michigan State University. We initiated contact with six firms, four of which agreed to participate. The participants were informed that the research was commissioned by the International Labor Organization (ILO), and the parties would have the right to review and comment on the report prior to submission to the ILO. Although the parties were given the right to keep their identities private, none opted for confidentiality.

Ultimately, we obtained access at four sites: Alcoa and United Steelworkers of America Local 4895, Rockdale, Texas; General Motors and United Automobile Workers (UAW) Local 652, Lansing, Michigan; Lear Corporation and UAW Local 1660, Elsie, Michigan; and Sparrow Health Systems and the Michigan Nurses Association, Lansing, Michigan. The sites, with their associated business characteristics, are listed in Table 4.1.

The sites represent a range of products, production processes, and market constraints. While each of these will be described in detail in the respective case studies, even this brief overview indicates that we were successful in obtaining sites that represented a range of production processes, product types, and market conditions. None of the sites are similar on these three dimensions.

On the other hand, we were less successful in obtaining geographic diversity. Three of the sites are in central southern Michigan. Two sites, General Motors–UAW Local 652 and Sparrow–Michigan Nurses Association, are in the same city, Lansing, Michigan. A third site, Lear Corporation–UAW Local 1660, is only 35 miles north of Lansing. We do not believe, however, that this geographic uniformity unduly compromises the generalization of the study. As will be seen, the GM–Lansing facility produces autos for an international market. Its unique characteristics are not due to its geographic location, but rather to its industrial history. Lear, as an auto supplier, is representative of auto suppliers, which tend to be concentrated in geographic areas proximate to automotive assembly plants, such as Michigan. Sparrow is subject to the same pressures as other health care organizations. Put differently, only Sparrow serves a primarily local or regional market, and servicing such a market is characteristic of health care organizations.

Table 4.1 General Characteristics of Sites in Study

Site	Product and process description	Product type	Market constraints	Location
Alcoa and United Steelworkers of America, Local 4895	Basic manufacturing (aluminum)	Commodity	Competitive global market, discrete number of potential customers; competitive oligopoly in product market	Rockdale, Texas
General Motors and UAW Local 652	Heavy assembly (automobiles)	Differentiated product	Internal choice within corporation for production; millions of potential national (and international) customers for product; competitive oligopoly in product market	Lansing, Michigan
Lear Corporation and UAW Local 1660	Light to medium assembly (motor vehicle parts, seating systems)	Moderately differentiated product made to customer specification	Discrete number of potential customers for product (oligopoly); competitive oligopoly in product market	Elsie, Michigan
Sparrow Health Systems	Health care (inpatient and outpatient services)	Service	Local/regional product market; limited number of competitive providers; choice generally made by third party (physician)	Lansing, Michigan

Nature of the Data to be Collected

The data collected were a mix of qualitative and quantitative data on collective bargaining at the site. The qualitative data were primarily a description by the parties of vehicles created by their collective bargaining systems to address issues of job protection/creation and competitiveness, the outcomes of the system. There was a focus on contractual structures, noncontractual formal structures, and informal programs. This was supported by obtaining descriptive contextual data on the nature of the production process (technological constraints) and the market constraints facing the site.

We also collected such basic quantitative data on employment trends since 1980, investment history, age of the facility, and numbers of strikes. While employment trends might be considered to be a key indicator of the extent to which the collective bargaining relationship has addressed employment protection and creation, one must be careful not to overinterpret the quantitative data based on a case study. We are unable to control for the other factors that may also affect employment. For example, employment may fall at a site because of declining industry demand, declining firm demand, or technological change, all factors that are largely independent of collective bargaining. It may be, however, that the collective bargaining system caused employment losses to be less than they would otherwise be. In such a case, collective bargaining protected jobs in an environment of declining employment. Strike incidence could be the result of a conflicting relationship between the parties at the plant, or of decisions made at higher levels of the company and union.

Given the variation in the case studies, the researchers did attempt to develop a definition of competitiveness to be imposed on the case studies. It was our expectation that each site would define competitiveness in its economic and market context. Competitiveness might be defined as a continually increasing market share in a growth industry; in a contracting industry, competitiveness might be defined as continuing existence.

Data Collection

Data collection was based on a structured interview from a generalized protocol, which attempted to learn about the interaction of collective bargaining, job security/creation, and competitiveness at the site. That general protocol is attached as an appendix to this chapter. Questions were also asked about the collective bargaining agreement. In addition, however, the researchers were given the flexibility to probe through the questions when the interview responses made it clear that the protocol may not capture the important components of the collective bargaining relationship. As the study attempted to gather data on the overall relationship, the researchers interviewed the key company and union officials who were responsible for the collective bargaining relationship. The number and identity of company and union officials were determined by each of the parties. The interviews were done in individual and group settings within parties, depending on the preferences of the parties. Any inconsistencies between the company and union officials were reported.

Most of the interviews occurred in 1999, during an upswing in the business cycle. Thus, the study takes the reader through the difficult economic period of the 1980s through the improved economic times of the 1990s. We do not consider the effect of the recent economic downturn.

Note

1. This differs from the situation in many European countries, for example, where employer associations and high-level union organizations, occasionally with government involvement, agree on minimum terms and conditions for all firms and employees covered by the association and the union.

References

Block, Richard N. 1990. "American Industrial Relations in the 1980s: Transformation or Evolution?" In *Reflections on the Transformation of Industrial Relations*, James Chelius and James Dworkin, eds. Metuchen, New Jersey, and London: IMLR Press/Rutgers University and Scarecrow Press, Inc., pp. 19–48.

Dunlop, John T. 1958. *Industrial Relations Systems*. Carbondale and Edwardsville, Illinois: Southern Illinois University Press.

Kochan, Thomas A., Harry C. Katz, and Robert B. McKersie. 1986. *The Transformation of American Industrial Relations*. New York: Basic Books.

Appendix

Date_____

Site_____

Interviewees: Name_____

Organization_____

Tentative Structure of Site Visit Protocol
for ILO Study

Michigan State University/ILO Study on Collective Bargaining,
Employment Protection/Creation and Competitiveness
January–March, 1999

Cluster I: Background of Plant and Local Union

A. Current situation
   Product
   Major customers
   Current employment level
      Supervisory
      Hourly
         P&M
         Clerical
         Others
B. Plant history (since 1980)
   Product history and current product
   Ownership history
   Age of the plant/Greenfield or Brownfield
   Collective bargaining/relationship history
   Employment trends
   Investment history
   Expansions
   Turnover in plant management
   Local union history
      Age of local
      Mergers of locals?
      Change in international?
   Relationship history
      No. of strikes
      Characterization by parties
         Conflictual, adversarial, cooperative, collaborative
         Third party involvement?

Cluster II: Competitive Pressures

When did you feel that your competitive environment had changed or that union members were faced with a new and different kind of threat to job security? These are distinct from the normal variations in employment and product demand associated with the business cycle.

What happened in your environment that sent you this message?

Cluster III: What Did You Do in Response to These Pressures?

A. We are looking for three basic types of responses/actions, etc.
  Changes in contract language
  Creation of formal structures that were not included in the contract
    Structures that operate regularly or on a recurring basis with specified systems
  Informal actions and programs
  Ad hoc, nonrecurring actions the parties took
B. What did you do and why did you do it?

Prototype Classification System

Action	Type	Competitiveness	Job Prot./Creation	Both
(Example) Wage freeze	Contract	x		
(Example) Layoff restrictions	Contract		x	
(Example) Productivity committee	Noncon. structure			x
(Example) Joint approach on tax abatement	Ad Hoc			x

Ask about the following if not mentioned:
  Wage freeze
  Reduced classifications
  Early retirement/attrition
  Different layoff system
  Outsourcing: restraints or removal of restraint
  Reduction in hours
  Wage reductions
  Two-tier wage system
      Length of time to convergence?
  Lump-sum payments (in lieu of wage increase)
  Neutrality pledge (for other plants)
  Retirement/new hire ratios
  Performance-based pay
      Profit-sharing
      Gain-sharing
      New incentive systems
  Investment in plant
  ESOP
  Creation of new structures
      Parallel union management structures for special purposes
      Task forces
      Committees
      New methods of negotiating
      Changes in processing grievances
      Jointly approaching government officials for aid (e.g., tax abatements)

Anything else?

C. Think about the things you did. Did you explicitly consider some types of actions and decide not to undertake those? Why did you choose actions you chose and reject the actions you did not choose?

D. What was the source of the change mechanism, e.g., how did you come to be aware of the possibility that these actions existed?
   Self-generated from people at the plant based on the relationship and experience (type of continuous improvement model)
   Formal experiments with evaluation
   Informal experiments (trial and error)
   Learning from others, but on your own (benchmarking)

Learning from experts
Private consultants
Books
Videos
Universities
Seminars and conferences
International union
Corporate staff

Cluster IV: Results

Did the changes achieve their desired objectives?
How do you know, what measures do you use?
Were there any unforeseen consequences?
Is there anything else you want to tell us that will aid in understanding
    your case?

5

Basic Aluminum

Alcoa–Rockdale, Texas, and United Steelworkers of America Local 4895

Richard N. Block
Michigan State University

DESCRIPTION OF THE BUSINESS

Alcoa Inc. is the world's largest producer of aluminum and alumina and fabricated products. It is involved in all segments of the industry: mining, refining, smelting, fabricating, and recycling. In 2000, following a 1999 merger with Reynolds, Alcoa had approximately 140,000 employees with 300 operating locations in 36 countries. In 2001, Alcoa had approximately 142,000 employees in 37 countries. Alcoa's 2001 revenues were U.S.$22.9 billion (Alcoa 2001).

Aluminum, an extremely abundant element, must be extracted from other substances. Bauxite is the basic physical raw material from which aluminum is obtained. Bauxite contains approximately 45 percent alumina, which is a powdery aluminum oxide that looks like white granulated sugar. After the alumina is removed from the bauxite, the aluminum and the oxygen are separated in an electrolytic reduction cell commonly called a "pot," in which the alumina is dissolved in molten cryolite and is reduced to metallic aluminum. The aluminum is then cast into large ingots or smaller molds called "hogs" or "pigs," which are suitable for remelting or fabricating (Alcoa 2001). This is called the aluminum smelting process. Plants that produce primary aluminum are commonly called smelters.

HISTORY OF THE FACILITY

Alcoa's Rockdale facility is located in Rockdale, Texas, a town of approximately 5,200. Rockdale is approximately 60 miles (100 kilometers) northeast of Austin and 144 miles (230 kilometers) northwest of Houston. The plant is a smelter, extracting aluminum from alumina, and also produces aluminum powder.

The plant's major customer is internal to Alcoa, an Alcoa flat-rolled aluminum plant in Davenport, Iowa. Among the major final customers for the aluminum produced at Rockdale are the aerospace industry and lithographic industry, which uses aluminum in lithographic plates. Aluminum powder is used in such products as deodorant, paint, metal pots, ordnance, and rocket fuels.

The Rockdale smelter was completed in 1952 as part of the United States' defense effort to maintain a large supply of aluminum for defense purposes. Electricity, the largest cost input to the aluminum manufacturing process, is used to provide power to run the facility and to extract the aluminum from the alumina. The smelter was located in Rockdale because of the presence of a large supply of lignite coal to provide electricity for the facility. There is a coal mine, called the Sandow Mine, that is adjacent to the Rockdale facility, and that provides coal to power the facility's electrical generators. Although Alcoa has always owned the mine and the power plant, until 1988–1989, Alcoa contracted the operation of the mine and power plant to the utility that served the Rockdale area. Alcoa has operated the mine since 1988, and the power plant since 1989.

It was believed that the Sandow Mine would provide a long-term supply of electricity. This was to be especially advantageous because it was believed in the early 1950s that the supply of electricity from water would soon peak, and other sources would be necessary. Although it is more costly to produce electricity from coal than from water, Alcoa believed that this cost disadvantage would be more than offset by adequate supplies of coal from the Sandow Mine.

Current employment (both salaried and hourly) at the site, including the mine, power plant, and smelter, is approximately 1,300. The peak employment at the site was approximately 2,000, reached in the early 1970s. As can be seen in Figure 5.1, this decline in employment

Figure 5.1 Employment in Primary Aluminum Industry, All Employees and Production Employees, 1973–2000

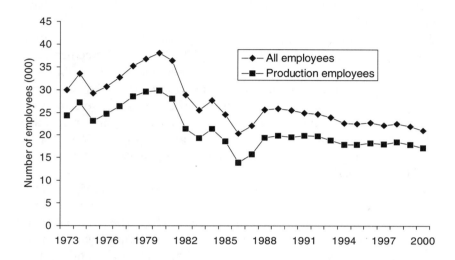

reflected the overall decline in employment in the primary aluminum industry in the United States over the past quarter of a century.

HISTORY AND BACKGROUND OF COLLECTIVE BARGAINING AT ROCKDALE

Of the 1,300 employees at Rockdale, 800 are hourly employees represented by United Steelworkers of America (USWA) Local 4895, 260 are power plant or mine employees represented by a local of another international union, and 240 are salaried and unrepresented. The focus of this case study is on the relationship between Local 4895 and Alcoa, although the relationship between Alcoa and the other local will be addressed as necessary.

Local 4895 was certified as the collective bargaining representative of the production and maintenance employees at Rockdale in 1953. In 2000, the employees represented by Local 4895 were covered by a master agreement between Alcoa and the international union, United Steelworkers of America covering plants in Badin, North Carolina; Alcoa (Knoxville), Tennessee; Bauxite, Arkansas; and Pt. Comfort, Texas, in addition to the Rockdale employees. The parties have generally had a harmonious relationship. The only exception was a 35-day strike in 1986, from June 1 to July 4, that was called among all employees represented under the Alcoa–USWA master agreement.

As a result of that strike, Alcoa obtained additional flexibility in combining classifications and, therefore, restructuring the way work was performed. Prior to 1986, more classification lines were in existence, and Alcoa could only assign employees outside their respective classifications on a voluntary basis. Following the work stoppage, employees were required to perform any assignment they were qualified to safely perform.

Overall, the relationship between Alcoa and Local 4895 is mature and cooperative. The parties arbitrate only one or two grievances per year, and these are primarily discharge cases. The parties have an expedited procedure for overtime grievances, minor discipline cases, and a few other issues, such as contracting out. The company has the right to subcontract; however, the parties are obligated to meet and discuss such needs before any decision is reached. Although the 1986 strike is still discussed, it does not appear to have affected the long-term relationship of the parties.

For many years, the USWA also benefited from the fact that labor accounts for only about 17 percent of the cost of aluminum. The most important cost in the production of aluminum is energy. In this sense, then, the unions reaped the benefits of the Marshallian condition of "the importance of being unimportant" (Kochan and Block 1977). Within broad limits, Alcoa could be generous with the unions representing its employees, because the major cost components were associated with inputs other than labor.

Indicative of Alcoa's labor relations strategy/philosophy is its relationship with the other local union at the Rockdale site. When Alcoa assumed operations of the power plant and mine in the late 1980s, it voluntarily recognized the other local union as the representative of the mine and power plant employees. Although Alcoa unsuccessfully requested that the National Labor Relations Board (NLRB) designate the mine and power plant as one unit, the decision did not affect the company's relationship with the other local.

COMPETITIVE PRESSURES

During the first three quarters of the twentieth century, Alcoa was the dominant player in the world aluminum market. Thus, during the period from the 1940s through the 1970s, Alcoa and its employees, like many other unionized firms in the United States, benefited from market dominance. Alcoa was able to pass on any cost increases that might be associated with collective bargaining.

This favorable situation began to turn in the early 1980s. Since then, the Rockdale plant has faced four major competitive issues. Each of these will be discussed.

Market Pressure

One major source of competitive pressure on Rockdale is the globalization of the market for aluminum. This has manifested itself in two ways: an increased supply of aluminum on the world market, and the development of a centralized, market-based pricing mechanism. Each of these will be examined.

Increased supply of aluminum

Since the early 1980s, there has been a globalization of the market for aluminum. Developed or emerging countries (such as China, following an import substitution policy) have established domestic aluminum-smelting operations which are throwing aluminum onto the world market. Russia for many years had an aluminum industry that serviced the defense needs of the Soviet Union during the cold war. Now that the cold war has ended and those defense needs no longer exist, the aluminum produced by the Russian capacity is being sent to the world market. In essence, the market for aluminum has become commoditized. Aluminum has become a commodity available from multiple sources at a world price determined primarily by supply and demand.

Commoditization has resulted in enormous variation in the price of aluminum. Some sense of this variation can be obtained by examining

Figure 5.2, which depicts the cash seller and settlement price of aluminum between July 1993 and March 1999. The price was at roughly U.S.$0.50 per pound (U.S.$1,000/ton) in late 1993. The price rose to well over U.S.$1.00 per pound (U.S.$2,200/ton) during the first quarter of 1995. Since then, there has been a general, albeit uneven trend downward to a March 1999 level of U.S.$0.58 per pound (U.S.$1,150/ton). This lack of price certainty has placed increasing cost pressure on the company, because Alcoa's revenue stream is less certain than it once was.

Information flows

A second major contributor toward commoditization was the emergence of the London Metal Exchange (LME) in the early 1980s as a facilitator of the market for nonferrous metals, including aluminum. Prior to the emergence of the exchange, Alcoa, as the largest aluminum producer in the world, could determine prices based on its cost struc-

Figure 5.2 Cash Seller and Settlement Price of Aluminum, July 1993–March 1999

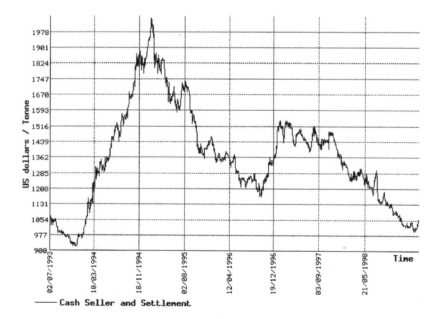

— Cash Seller and Settlement

SOURCE: London Metal Exchange (www.lme.co.uk).

ture. The LME created a market mechanism for pricing. Thus, Alcoa now had to accept the world price of aluminum, a price that was independent of its costs.

Cost Pressure from Environmental Regulations

The third source of competitive pressure on the Rockdale facility is from increased environmental regulations in the 1980s, primarily the Clean Air Act. The power plant generates and the smelter uses electricity from coal, and coal creates emissions that must be cleaned. In addition, the Sandow Mine is a strip mine, and the land must be reclaimed and restored to an appearance as close as possible to its pre-mining state. Although some of these regulations have encouraged waste reduction—and therefore cost reduction—in general, environmental regulations require expenditures without a rate of return. The smelter sees them as purely a cost. To the extent that the environmental regulations impose additional costs on the production process over and above what the company would otherwise directly incur to produce the aluminum, there is pressure on the collective bargaining system to be the source of the offset of those costs.

Cost Pressure from Use of Coal

When the decision was made in 1952 to locate the Rockdale smelter near the coal seam, it was believed that smelter sites near relatively inexpensive hydro-generated electricity would soon be exhausted. This has not been the case. The parties estimate that coal-generated electricity costs three times as much as water-generated electricity. As with environmental regulations, there is constant pressure on the collective bargaining system to offset this cost disadvantage.

COLLECTIVE BARGAINING, COMPETITIVENESS, AND EMPLOYMENT PROTECTION/CREATION

Since the mid 1980s, management and the employees at Rockdale have become increasingly aware of the importance of plant competitiveness and job protection. Plant management began to emphasize competitiveness in the mid 1980s, as indicated by its insistence during the 1986 strike on increased flexibility to assign workers to tasks. The parties have generally had a cooperative, high-trust relationship. Therefore, when the company began to raise issues of competitiveness with the union, and ultimately job security, the union took them seriously and was willing to cooperate. The union leadership also saw consistency between the company's competitiveness/job security message and reports in the general news media regarding globalization and competitiveness.

Contract Changes

As one of five plants under the master Alcoa–USWA agreement, the parties at Rockdale are somewhat constrained in their actions. Given this, it is not surprising the parties' main tool for addressing competitiveness and job security has been a traditional one, wage restraint in the collective agreement. Wage data provided by the company for a representative group of pay grades indicate that between 1977 and 1986, the average base wage increased by 62 percent, from approximately $8.08 per hour to $13.12 per hour. From 1986 to 1996, however, the average base wage of those classifications increased only 9 percent, from $13.12 to $14.32.

It should be noted, however, that this 9 percent increase masks increases associated with combining of job classifications. When the job classifications in the new grouping were upgraded, the wage rates in the previously lower-paid classifications were increased to the level of the higher-paid classifications in the grouping. Many employees received wage increases associated with this upgrading. In addition, employees have benefited from an increase in variable compensation, such as profit sharing. A reduction in job classification and enhanced management flexibility to assign work, provided employees are qualified, was important to plant management as it gave them increased flexibility to assign employees.

The parties also increased the length of the master contract from the usual three years, to six years. Although there was a reopener in 2001, unresolved issues were submitted to binding arbitration. This provided the company with increased stability in its production planning and cost structure.

Noncontractual Formal Structures

The major structural noncontractual innovation has been the creation of partnership teams. The impetus for the teams came from corporate level and the international union, who directed that all plants covered by the Alcoa–Steelworkers master agreement undertake some sort of initiative, primarily to upgrade the skills of the workforce. The parties at Rockdale used this directive to create partnership teams at the plant and department levels. The plant-level partnership team consists of the plant manager, the labor relations staff, all department heads, and the union bargaining committee. Each department in the smelter also has a partnership team that sends representatives to the plant-level team.

The union sees the purpose of the partnership team as improving the position of the Rockdale plant in the market. At the same time, it is advantageous to employees to have a say in how the plant is run. From the company's point of view, the benefit of the partnership team is the improvement of employee productivity, leading to improving relative market position.

The partnership team has been the vehicle through which the Alcoa Production System, Alcoa's version of the modern demand-driven production system, is being implemented at Rockdale. In the ingot plant, union and management came together to reorganize scrap handling, saving hundreds of thousands of dollars per year by recycling scrap that had previously not been recycled. Similar successful efforts have been made in the pot room and the carbon plant. These efforts have reduced costs, thereby increasing the competitiveness of the plant. Hourly and supervisory employees have been sent to seminars and conferences both inside and outside Alcoa to aid them in instituting the system. They have also been sent to other Alcoa facilities for benchmarking purposes.

The parties cited several changes that would not have occurred but for the existence of the partnership team. These have involved the return of work that had once been contracted out, or retention of work that was scheduled to be contracted out. For example, the plant has a yard service that acts like a construction crew. The yard service had been short-staffed and unable to perform needed work. Through the efforts of the partnership team, seven people were added to the yard service, and it began doing construction that had been previously contracted out. This solution upgraded the skills of the workforce and permitted the represented employees to do work for which Alcoa was paying a great deal. Because of the upgrading of the workforce, the cost differential between the contractors' employees and the unionized employees declined. Thus, jobs were protected through the partnership team, encouraging the reassignment of people.

In 1997, the plant management was considering contracting out its janitorial function of six to eight employees. The matter came to the attention of the partnership team. Under the auspices of the team, the parties developed a proposal to reschedule and redistribute the janitorial work, including adding weekend work that could be done without disrupting the normal production. The result was that the original janitorial jobs were retained and four additional janitorial jobs were created. The retention of the janitorial jobs in the plant also had the unintended benefit of creating some less physically demanding positions that could be filled by employees with physical restrictions.

Through the partnership team, the local union president was also assigned 40 hours per week to union-management issues, and granted office space in a centrally located area. This has permitted the union to increase its awareness of all issues in the plant, as compared to the situation that would exist if the local president had assigned duties and could respond only as contacted by employees.

Ad Hoc Informal Structures

There are also important informal systems that are created at the plant. For example, there is a toolbox meeting at the beginning of each shift at which hourly employees and the supervisor discuss any issues that have arisen, particularly safety, Alcoa's top internal priority. As needed, employees have been released from their jobs for specified periods of time to develop training programs. This was done when job classifications were combined following the 1986 negotiations, and employees were required to be cross-trained in different crafts. In addition, as another example of informal, ad hoc action, the plant management and local union joined together to successfully lobby their U.S. Congressman in opposition to a tax on carbon-based fuel that could have threatened the existence of the plant, which depends on coal for so much of its power.

CONCLUSIONS

Alcoa–Rockdale and Steelworkers Local 4895 have what may be defined as a mature, traditional collective bargaining relationship. This is based to a large extent on Alcoa's corporate philosophy of respect for the institution of collective bargaining and a willingness to recognize the legitimacy of the unions, including the USWA, in the facilities where the employees have chosen union representation.

There is a high level of trust between the parties, and this has facilitated the use of the collective bargaining relationship to enhance both employment protection/creation and firm competitiveness. The long-time willingness of the company to provide the union with information on the state of the business and the facility, and the willingness of the union to accept that information at face value, was an important first step in adapting the relationship to the twin needs of employment protection/creation and competitiveness.

Initial responses to these two issues came not through specialized structures designed to address employment protection/creation and competitiveness, but rather through the traditional vehicle of the collective agreement and day-to-day informal interactions. Through the agreement the parties agreed on wage restraint, the introduction of variable compensation, a six-year contract with an arbitrated wage reopener, reduced job classifications, and flexibility in assignments. Ad hoc arrangements through interactions included toolbox discussions and safety committees.

As can be seen, the parties' mutual trust placed them in a position where they could move away from rights-based formalism based on management rights and union use of the grievance procedure to an interest-based relationship. It was not necessary to create structures or use external consultants to do this. The interest-based relationship simply flowed from the nature of the collective bargaining relationship.

When the formal competitiveness structure, the partnership team, was mandated in 1996, the parties had no difficulty incorporating it into their relationship. The partnership team mandate provided a formal vehicle for doing what the parties had been doing in any event. It was easy for them to adapt to this new system.

Anecdotes suggest that there have been specific instances in which the collective bargaining relationship contributed to job creation (such as yard service and janitorial function). The plant continues to operate profitably. The parties are aware of their common situation in Rockdale, and they will continue to do what is necessary to keep the plant competitive in an increasingly uncertain and competitive aluminum market.

The Alcoa Rockdale–Steelworkers Local 4895 case represents an excellent example of how value-based employment drives collective bargaining. With aluminum prices declining, or at least uncertain, the revenue stream associated with the product produced by the employees was declining, or at least less certain than it was in the past. That declining and/or uncertain revenue stream was the chief threat to the employees' jobs. In the absence of legal job security guarantees in the United States, the union must depend on itself to address job security. At Rockdale, this took the form of cooperation with the company to increase the cost-competitiveness of the plant by reducing the cost of producing aluminum. Job security and firm competitiveness then were seen as one and the same.

Notes

In addition to the interviewees cited in this chapter, the authors would like to thank Ms. Janine Fogg, formerly with Alcoa; Mr. Greg Freehling, Alcoa; Ms. Colleen Haley, Alcoa–Fujikura; and Mr. Jim Michaud, Alcoa–Fujikura, for their cooperation in this research. Mr. Joe Quaglia, manager of human resources–industrial relations, and Ms. Joyce Saltzman and Ms. Bonita Cersomino of Alcoa Corporate Communications provided important comments that enhanced the accuracy of the chapter.

Unless otherwise noted parenthetically in the text, the material in this chapter is based on interviews with Anders et al. (1999), Carney (1999), and Cleveland et al. (1999).

References

Alcoa. 2001. Web site, <http://www.alcoa.com>.

Anders, Lloyd, retired officer, United Steelworkers of America Local 4895; Bill Eckert, manager, power and mining, Alcoa–Rockdale; Larry Nolen, president, United Steelworkers of America Local 4895, Stephen Srnensky, vice president, United Steelworkers of America Local 4895; joint interview, March 11, 1999.

Carney, Dennis, plant manager, Alcoa Rockdale, conversation, March 11, 1999.

Cleveland, Joe, safety and training superintendent, Alcoa–Rockdale; Jon Cook, labor relations superintendent, Alcoa–Rockdale; Matt Everitt, Ingot plant superintendent, Alcoa–Rockdale; Bob Turner, personnel superintendent, Alcoa–Rockdale; joint interview, March 11, 1999.

Kochan, Thomas A., and Richard N. Block. 1977. "An Interindustry Analysis of Bargaining Outcomes: Preliminary Evidence from Two-Digit Industries." *Quarterly Journal of Economics* 91(3): 431–452.

6
Auto Assembly

General Motors–Lansing, Michigan, and United Automobile Workers Local 652

Richard N. Block
Peter Berg
Michigan State University

DESCRIPTION OF THE BUSINESS

General Motors (GM) in Lansing, Michigan, consists of four divisions, the employees of which are represented by UAW Local 652: Worldwide Facilities, which consists of skilled trades, primarily construction; Powertrain, which is responsible for designing and building engines and transmissions for GM vehicles; metal fabrication, which is responsible for sheet metal; and small car assembly, which is responsible for the actual assembly of the vehicles. As of October 2001, the Lansing facilities assembled the Pontiac Grand Am, the Oldsmobile Alero, and the Chevrolet Malibu. The Grand Am is an established nameplate that has been restyled several times over the last decade. It has long been one of GM's most successful vehicles. The Alero is a new nameplate, and the Malibu is a revived nameplate. Lansing and Lordstown, Ohio, which is also part of GM small car assembly, are the main assembly locations for GM small cars. Saturn, in Spring Hill, Tennessee, also assembles small cars, but under a different agreement.

Also located in Lansing are a body plant, a parts facility, and the Craft Centre, which manufactures GM's electric car and the Chevrolet Cavalier and Pontiac Sunfire convertibles. The production employees in these facilities are represented by UAW locals other than Local 652.

HISTORY OF THE SITE

Lansing is a medium-sized city with a 2000 population of 119,128 (U.S. Bureau of the Census 2001a) in the midst of a metropolitan area with a 2000 population of 447,728 (U.S. Bureau of the Census, 2001b). The city is located in southern lower Michigan, approximately 90 miles northwest of Detroit. Other major employers in the area are the State of Michigan (Lansing is the state capital) and Michigan State University.

Oldsmobile was founded as an automobile producer in Lansing in 1897 by Ransom Olds. After GM acquired Oldsmobile in 1908, Lansing became the headquarters of the Oldsmobile division of GM. Until the early 1980s, Lansing was a complete automotive manufacturing complex—a hometown manufacturer. Oldsmobile maintained power-train, sheet metal, parts, and assembly facilities in Lansing. GM's body division, Fisher Body, also maintained a plant that supplied Oldsmobile with car bodies. Through the 1970s and early 1980s, Oldsmobile manufactured mid-size and full-size rear-wheel-drive automobiles in Lansing: the Oldsmobile Cutlass Supreme, a mid-size two-door automobile; the Oldsmobile 88, a full-size automobile; and the Oldsmobile 98, a luxury automobile.

With a corporate reorganization in 1983–1984, which is discussed in the following section, GM chose to establish Lansing as a manufacturing site for small front-wheel-drive vehicles. Because Lansing had been tooled to assemble large, rear-wheel-drive vehicles, GM invested approximately U.S.$40–$60 million in Lansing by building a new paint plant, a new assembly plant, and remodeling the fabrication facilities. From the mid 1980s through the late 1990s, GM Lansing and Local 652 assembled the Pontiac Grand Am (three major styling changes), the Buick Skylark (two major styling changes), the Oldsmobile Calais, the Chevrolet Cavalier, and the Oldsmobile Achieva.

EMPLOYMENT AT GM–LANSING

GM employment in Lansing facilities represented by Local 652 peaked at approximately 15,000 hourly and salaried employees in

1980. Overall, Lansing facilities employment has been reduced primarily due to corporate reorganizations that will be discussed below, as well as by a 1995 decision to move to Detroit engineering and marketing personnel who had been in Lansing. At the end of 2000, the employment level in the four Lansing divisions in which Local 652 represents was approximately 8,600 skilled and nonskilled workers and 2,500 salaried workers. In 2000, the average age of the workforce was 46, indicating little turnover, which is to be expected in a high-wage industry.

Each year the Lansing divisions hire between 200 and 300 workers (many of which are interplant transfers from other GM facilities). External candidates are hired based on the recommendations of current GM employees. It was estimated that about half of the employees in the Lansing divisions were hired through family referrals or have family working for GM.

The decline in production worker employment in Lansing has tracked the general drop in unionized auto employment in the United States since the early 1980s and GM's declining market share. Figures 6.1 and 6.2 demonstrate this trend. Figure 6.1 graphs overall production employment and unionized employment in the motor vehicle and equipment industry from 1983–2000. The production employment and unionized data are from different sources. The production employment data are from establishment data collected by the Current Employment Statistics, and union membership data are from individual data collected by the Current Population Survey.

Despite the unmatched data, the results are interesting. In 1983, the number of production workers and the number of union members was almost identical—568,000. Between 1984 and 1986, the number of union members exceeded the number of production workers. This is most likely because many unionized workers on layoff as a result of the economic slowdown in the industry reported themselves as union members, although part of this could be due to data differences. By 1987, however, the trend that would persist throughout 1990s had begun: a long-term increase in the number of production workers in the industry, and a long-term decrease in the number of union members. This was the result of foreign-owned firms (Toyota, Nissan, BMW, Daimler Benz) opening non-union facilities in the United States, as well as the increase in non-union auto parts suppliers (Cutcher-Gersh-

**Figure 6.1 Production Employees and Union Members, Motor Vehicles
and Equipment, 1983–2000**

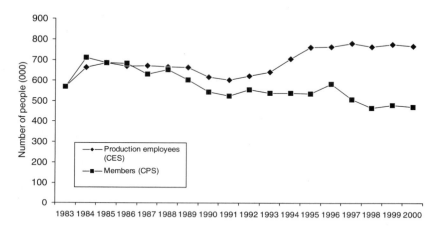

NOTE: CES = data came from Current Employment Statistics; CPS = data came from
Current Population Survey.
SOURCE: Hirsch and McPherson (1994); U.S. Bureau of Labor Statistics, Current
Employment Statistics, National Employment and Hours Earnings, Motor Vehicles
and Equipment.

enfeld and McHugh 1994). These results are supported by unionization
estimates displayed in Figure 6.2, which shows unionization in motor
vehicles and equipment declining as a percentage of all employees and
as a percentage of production employees.

In addition to these overall industry trends, GM–Lansing and
Local 652 were affected by trends in GM's market share. General
Motors saw its share of the U.S. motor vehicle market decline from 46
percent in 1978 to approximately 29 percent in 2000 (Fox 1996; Flint
1998; *Automotive News* 2001a,b; Henry 2001).

Figure 6.2 Union Membership and Collective Bargaining Coverage as a Percentage of Production Employees and Total Employees, Motor Vehicles and Equipment, 1983–2000

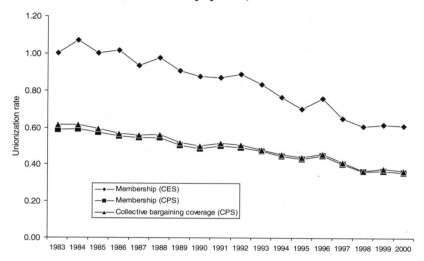

NOTE: CES = data came from Current Employment Statistics; CPS = data came from Current Population Survey.

SOURCE: Hirsch and McPherson (1994); U.S. Bureau of Labor Statistics, Current Employment Statistics, National Employment and Hours Earnings, Motor Vehicles and Equipment.

HISTORY AND BACKGROUND OF COLLECTIVE BARGAINING AT GM–LANSING

Local 652 was originally chartered circa 1937, when GM recognized the UAW as the collective bargaining representative of the production employees in its plants. Two groups of workers have severed from the local, one when the parts division was established and one when the Craft Centre was established.

Since the late 1930s, GM and the UAW have negotiated a master agreement for all GM plants. That agreement and supporting documents provide the basic terms and conditions of employment for all GM hourly employees. The national agreement establishes such corporate-wide provisions as guidelines for wage levels and wage increases, by wage range, benefits, interplant transfer rights, and specified employment rights of covered employees. GM–Lansing and Local 652, as with all GM facilities, negotiates a local agreement to determine which classifications are in specified wage ranges and to address such plant-level issues as seniority, job transfer, shift preference, and work practices.

The relationship between then–Oldsmobile Division of GM and currently GM–Lansing and UAW Local 652 has long been traditional but peaceful. The accordant nature of the relationship between GM–Lansing and Local 652 is indicated by the fact that there has never been a local strike in Lansing. By contrast, for example, since 1996 GM has experienced local strikes in Flint, Michigan; Janesville, Wisconsin; and Dayton, Ohio (Bradsher 1996, 1998; Livingston 1996). Although there is an arbitration provision in the national agreement, there have been no arbitrations in Lansing since the 1970s.

COMPETITIVE PRESSURES

General Motors–Lansing and UAW Local 652 have been affected by two key environmental factors since the mid 1980s: the changing nature of the automobile market, and GM corporate reorganization. In addition, there are two factors that are specific to Lansing: the nature of the product, and the production process that affected the competitive situation. Each of these will be examined.

Changing Nature of the Automobile Market

The change in the U.S. automobile market has been so heavily documented in the business press that it is unnecessary to address it here in any detail. These changes had a severe effect on GM, especially the long-term decline in GM's share of the U.S. motor vehicle market. The parties were also affected by the closing of GM plants in California. The message was clear: the days in which GM dominated the U.S. automobile market had ended.

General Motors Corporate Reorganization

During the period 1983–1984, GM undertook one of the most extensive reorganizations in its corporate history. Since the 1920s, GM had been organized based on distinct divisions and nameplates, each of which designed, manufactured, and marketed its own vehicles. Although each of these vehicles was designed to capture a different price segment of the market (in order from lowest priced to highest priced: Chevrolet, Pontiac, Oldsmobile, Buick, Cadillac), there were overlapping models within brand names. Thus, there was some competition among brands. During this time, Oldsmobile was a full-line manufacturing division. As the "hometown" for Oldsmobile, Lansing would always produce Oldsmobiles.

The reorganization changed this. With the reorganization, the former design and manufacturing divisions would now become simply marketing divisions, promoting the vehicles GM produced. Although the vehicles would still be called Oldsmobiles, they could be manufactured anywhere within the GM system, including Lansing. Additionally, any other nameplate could also be manufactured anywhere in the GM system, including Lansing.

In other words, the manufacturing facilities in Lansing were decoupled from Oldsmobile and assigned to GM. Prior to the decoupling, as long as Oldsmobile was a full-line manufacturing division, Lansing would always have product to build because these were Oldsmobile manufacturing facilities. Once Oldsmobile became simply a marketing division, with manufacturing decisions made separately, Lansing would only obtain work that GM allocated to it. Lansing could lose Oldsmobile work, and it could gain non-Oldsmobile work. The Lansing facilities and other GM plants would hereafter depend on GM for product allocation.

This reorganization caused uncertainty for the GM–Lansing employees and UAW Local 652. General Motors products/models generally have a life cycle of five to six years. There would never be a guarantee of product after a vehicle line produced in Lansing was dropped. Because GM does not guarantee product allocations to plants, Lansing, like other GM manufacturing facilities, would be required to constantly compete for vehicles to assemble. Lansing was now required to compete for GM production work, rather than simply operate as the manufacturing arm of Oldsmobile.

The Nature of the Product

With the reorganization, GM chose to establish Lansing as a manufacturing site for small cars. In the mid 1980s, GM was unable to turn a profit on its small vehicles. General Motors continued to market and produce small vehicles, however, because of the requirement that the company maintain a high average corporate fuel economy (CAFE) standard. The small cars generated high mileage, raising GM's overall average and permitting the company to continue to market and produce larger, less fuel-efficient—but profitable—vehicles.

This product, then, placed pressure on GM–Lansing and Local 652 to reduce costs so that the vehicles produced in Lansing could be profitable. General Motors would likely continue to increase the efficiency of its larger vehicles and to pressure the government for relief from CAFE. To the extent it was successful in either or both of these endeavors, the need to produce unprofitable small cars in Lansing would be reduced; thus, the incentive for GM–Lansing and UAW Local 652 was to make small cars profitable for GM.

The Production Process

Although GM's investment modernized the assembly process in Lansing, the body plant is three miles from the main assembly facilities. As a result, GM must truck bodies from the body plant to the assembly plant. This placed (and continues to place) the Lansing assembly process at an inherent cost disadvantage vis-à-vis other plants inside and outside GM at which the body facility and the assembly plant are adjacent to one another.

COLLECTIVE BARGAINING, COMPETITIVENESS, AND EMPLOYMENT PROTECTION/CREATION

Contractual Structures

As noted, GM and the international union, UAW, have negotiated a national agreement for all GM hourly workers, including employees represented by Local 652. The 1996 and 1999 national agreements included a Job Security (JOBS) Program. The JOBS program provides for Secured Employment Levels (SELs) for each bargaining unit equal to the number of active employees with at least one year of seniority and prohibits layoffs for any reason other than sales declines, acts of God or other reasons beyond the control of the corporation, sale of part of the business, if another employee is recalled or assigned to a temporary position, or if there is model change or plant rearrangement. As stated in an agreement between General Motors Corp. and UAW, November 2, 1996, the SEL is reduced by attrition, and employees whose jobs are eliminated may avail themselves of interplant transfer rights. The JOBS program provides for substantial job security for UAW Local 652–represented employees, and creates an incentive for the parties to make the most efficient use of employees as a generally fixed asset.

Noncontractual Structures

In order to fully understand the collective bargaining system in Lansing and the relationship between this system and competitiveness and employment protection/creation, one must understand the noncontractual structures the parties have created. In addition, one must understand the physical nature of GM production in Lansing.

Jointness

Noncontractual jointness permeates the relationship. Every possible function, such as health and safety, communications, and ergonomics has a plant management and union representative assigned to it. Each of the plant functional representatives reports to a local union official with local-wide responsibility for that function. These functional representatives, in turn, report to a joint activities chair through a monthly meeting. The joint activities chair reports to the chair of the bargaining committee. Through this structure, everything that affects Local 652–represented employees is jointly administered. There are very few employee-related decisions that management makes without union involvement.

This labor–management system creates consistency across the four divisions. Prior to the reorganization, all functions in Lansing reported to Oldsmobile. This local autonomy of Oldsmobile in Lansing helped to create consistency; everybody was building Oldsmobiles. When the corporation reorganized, each plant manager had different divisional reporting lines, e.g., Powertrain reported to corporate Powertrain, assembly reported to corporate small car assembly, and metal fabrication reported to corporate metal fabrication. But Local 652 and the GM–Lansing (formerly Oldsmobile) labor relations system remained unitary across all divisions.

This system is called the "star system" by the chair of the local bargaining committee. At the hub of the star sits Local 652 and GM–Lansing labor relations. Each point of the star represents a different function that union and management undertake jointly on a site-wide basis, such as outsourcing, health and safety, communications, and ergonomics. Although organizationally each of the four divisions in Lansing reports to different corporate heads, as noted, the labor relations function is unitary across all four divisions, reporting to GM–Lansing Labor Relations. All the hourly employees in each division are represented by Local 652, and there is one labor relations function across all four divisions. As the supervisor of labor relations for the site stated in the interview, "Nothing goes on in the plants that I don't know about."

Scale

A second key characteristic of the labor relations system in Lansing is size and scale. This scale provides the opportunity for employee movement across all four divisions depending on the needs of the division, and the unified labor relations systems across the four divisions provide the means for employee movement. If there are excess employees in one division because of short-term production variations, these employees can be easily shifted to another division because all divisions are represented by the same local, and the labor relations function for all divisions is unitary. In a sense, Lansing has created a small-scale Japanese-type system of affiliated corporations in which the affiliates help the main corporation by absorbing excess workers when needed, thereby maintaining employment.

Examples

This labor relations system serves to maintain the connection between the otherwise separate divisions and ensures consistency of labor relations across all the divisions. It also ensures that the independent plant managers who report to corporate stay firmly anchored in the Lansing collective bargaining system. Three examples illustrate how the system works toward competitiveness and employment protection/creation. First, because the parties worked together so well, since the mid 1990s, GM has turned a profit on each Lansing-built automobile it sells. This was accomplished by the parties working together to consistently take costs out of the vehicle. This was a major change for Lansing because, as noted, their position was precarious so long as GM was losing money on its small cars. There was no structure explicitly dedicated to making the vehicle profitable. All the parties realized the need and did what was necessary.

An example of employment protection is illustrated by an anecdote regarding sign fabrication. Several years ago, a fabrication divisional manufacturing manager decided to outsource the fabrication of signs to be used within the plant, as he wanted the signs in all corporate fabricating plants to be the same. The manager was informed by GM–Lansing labor relations and Local 652 that sign manufacture was not outsourced in Lansing, that skilled tradespeople built signs, and that Local 652–represented employees would be willing to make the signs to the divisional manager's specifications. In this case, the plant manager simply failed to consider the fact that a broader labor relations system existed in Lansing, and that his plant was part of the "home-town" system.

A third example involves the production of camshafts. GM–Powertrain wanted to put a camshaft line in Lansing. General Motors attempted to dictate how the line would be built and installed, but the Lansing plant said that it would be built by toolmakers, electricians, and machine repairpersons, because "this is the way it is done in Lansing." The camshafts were built to specification and at the target cost, but they were built and installed with the configuration of workers that was customary in Lansing, protecting the jobs of Lansing employees.

In January 2000, GM announced that it would build a $558 million auto assembly plant in Lansing, at the site where the main assembly plant has been located. Called Lansing Grand River Assembly, the plant is GM's first new assembly plant in 15 years. Starting in late 2001, this plant, staffed by members of Local 652, will build the next generation of the Cadillac Catera, the Cadillac CTS, a GM vehicle for the entry-level luxury market. More important, however, this investment means it is likely that Local 652 will have work and jobs for years into the future. This means long-term job security for the Lansing workforce (Evanoff 2000; Vlasic 2000).[1]

CONCLUSIONS

The Lansing collective bargaining system is based on a unitary labor relations function across otherwise independent GM divisions, Local 652–representation of hourly employees in all four divisions, formal and deep jointness, and scale. By the only criterion that really matters for plant management and a local union, product allocation by GM, the Lansing system has been successful in both creating a competitive production system and protecting jobs in Lansing, and doing it within the limits of GM's long-term market share decline and the overall production employment decline in the U.S. unionized sector. Since the mid 1980s, GM has continued to allocate small car production to the Lansing site. More important for the future employment, however, GM has made substantial capital investment in Lansing, including its newest assembly plant, Lansing Grand River Assembly. Working with state-of-the-art capital and production systems is likely to make GM–Lansing extremely competitive in the future. GM–Lansing and Local 652 are likely to continue to be allocated product, thereby maximizing employment opportunities for Local 652 members. Given declining market share and declining employment, a local is successful in this system if it is able to minimize large employment losses by obtaining GM investment and product allocation. By this measure, the relationship has been successful with respect to both employment and competitiveness.

Equally important for GM–Lansing and Local 652 is the diversification of its product line. With the allocation of the Cadillac CTS to Lansing, GM–Lansing and Local 652 now assemble a product that is likely to generate higher margins than the small cars produced in Lansing in the 1980s and 1990s. Thus, the margins of the overall Lansing product mix should improve, further enhancing Lansing's standing in the GM hierarchy.

It appears that the long-term relationship between GM and UAW Local 652 was an essential element in a substantial GM investment in production capacity in Lansing. This indicates that GM believes it can competitively produce vehicles in Lansing. Equally important, it would confirm the success of GM–Lansing labor relations and UAW Local 652 in creating a system that is competitive for the corporation and maximizes employment opportunities for GM employees represented by UAW Local 652.

The collective bargaining system created by GM–Lansing and UAW Local 652 has been extremely successful in bargaining under the constraints of the U.S. collective bargaining and employment relations systems. The location of Lansing Grand River Assembly gives UAW Local 652 the opportunity to work with the newest manufacturing technology and the most productive capital stock in the GM system, thus maximizing the value created by Local 652 employees.

Notes

In addition to the interviewees cited in the report, the authors would like to thank Mr. Fred Charles, joint activities representative, UAW Local 652, and Mr. Michael Reinerth, human resources director, GM–Lansing Craft Centre, for their support in providing access to officials from UAW Local 652 and GM–Lansing; Mr. John Couthen Jr., supervisor, labor relations, Small Car Group, North American Operations, GM, Mr. Matthew W. Boyle, manager, industrial relations, Lansing Site, GM, and Mr. Ralph Sheppard, president, UAW Local 652, for their cooperation in this research; and Ms. Betty Barrett, Ph.D. candidate, School of Labor and Industrial Relations, Michigan State University, for her research assistance.

Unless otherwise noted parenthetically in the text, the material in this chapter is based on Baker and Scheffler (1999).

1. The Cadillac CTS exceeded GM's expectations in sales (Hayes 2002). In 2004, GM will add a second high-margin vehicle to the Lansing Grand River Assembly

product line—the Cadillac SRX, a "cross-over" sedan/sport utility vehicle. This addition will result in 700 new jobs in Lansing (Hayes 2003).

References

Automotive News. 2001a. "Market Data Book: U.S. Domestic and Imported Car Sales, 2000." Available at <http://www.autonews.com/page.cms?pageId=140>.

———. 2001b. "Market Data Book: U.S. Domestic and Imported Truck Sales, 2000." Available at <http://www.autonews.com/page.cms?pageId=140>.

Baker, Art, chair of the Shop Committee, United Auto Workers Local 652, and Bill Scheffler, supervisor of labor relations, Lansing Site, GM, joint interview, February 1, 1999.

Bradsher, Keith. 1996. "New Union Contract Lets G.M. Trim Some Labor Costs." *New York Times*, November 3.

———. 1998. "General Motors and U.A.W. Agree on End to Strike." *New York Times,* July 29.

Cutcher-Gershenfeld, Joel, and Patrick P. McHugh. 1994. "Collective Bargaining in the North American Auto Supply Industry." In *Contemporary Collective Bargaining in the Private Sector*, Paul Voos, ed. Madison, Wisconsin: Industrial Relations Research Association, pp. 225–258.

Evanoff, Ted. 2000. "GM to Build Factory with Flexibility." *Detroit Free Press*, Internet edition, January 31.

Flint, Jerry. 1998. "Panic Time at GM." *Forbes* 161(10): 80.

Fox, Justin. 1996. "The UAW Makes Nice." *Fortune* 134(8): 28.

Hayes, Lori. 2002. "CTS Takes off from the Cadillac Pack." *Lansing State Journal*, July 6. Available at <http://www.lsj.com/news/business/p_020706_cts_1a-5a.html>.

———. 2003. "Flex Time at GM." *Lansing State Journal*, January 5. Available at <http://www.lsj.com/news/business/030105_cflex_le-62.html>.

Henry, Jim. 2001. "Imports Take More Share from Big 3." *Automotive News*, January 8, p. 39.

Hirsch, Barry T., and David A. McPherson. 1994. *Union Membership and Earnings Data Book 1993: Compilations from the Current Population Survey*. Washington, DC: Bureau of National Affairs.

Livingston, Sandra. 1996. "Lordstown UAW to Vote on Pacts." *Cleveland Plain Dealer,* December 10.

U.S. Bureau of the Census. 2001a. "American Factfinder: DP-1. Profile of General Demographic Characteristics: 2000 Data Set: Census 2000 Sum-

mary File 1 (SF 1) 100-Percent Data Geographic Area: Lansing City."
Available at <http://factfinder.census.gov/servlet/BasicFactsServlet>.

———. 2001b. *Ranking Tables for Metropolitan Areas: Population in 2000 and Population Change from 1990 to 2000 (PHC-T-3)*. Washington, DC: U.S. Bureau of the Census.

Vlasic, Bill. 2000. "GM Opens Plant for New Era." *Detroit News*, Internet edition, January 31.

7
Automobile Parts

Lear Corporation–Elsie, Michigan, Division and United Automobile Workers Local 1660

Michael L. Moore
Richard N. Block
Michigan State University

The Lear Corporation's plant in Elsie, Michigan, and its union partner, Local 1660 of the United Automobile Workers (UAW) International Union, graphically illustrate global and national forces at play in reaching the goals of remaining competitive while providing for employment protection and job creation. Although the Lear Corporation in the aggregate is a conglomerate business with sales of over U.S.$5.9 billion, each of its auto component plants faces strong pressures from the corporation to demonstrate economic viability and advantage. It also faces pressures from its community to maintain or increase its employment base. The story of this rural plant and its employees' 35-year journey to remain open and to continue to be awarded new product placements is a typical yet fascinating story for a U.S. firm.

The Lear–Elsie and UAW Local 1660 case demonstrates the ability of collective bargaining practices and noncontractual workplace processes to cope with changing manufacturing paradigms. Between its opening in 1966 and the present, this plant has exemplified three manufacturing models. From 1966 to 1996, the Lear plant was a typical mass production facility. From 1996 to 2000, the plant shifted to a team-based work system closely aligned with the sociotechnical systems model. With the adoption of the 2000 contract with UAW Local 1660, the plant transformed itself into a lean production plant based on the principles of the Toyota Production System (Ohno 1988). The presentation of these contextual factors will be elaborated in the final sections of this chapter, as case findings are augmented with current

(2001) interview data. Attention now turns to the fundamentals of the business, the facility, the collective bargaining relationship, and the pressures toward competition and employment protection/creation at Lear–Elsie.

DESCRIPTION OF THE BUSINESS

The Lear–Elsie plant is part of Lear Corporation, an automotive components supplier. Lear's goal is to supply every component of an automobile interior in kitted modules suitable for assembly by major automotive producers. The corporation's worldwide sales were U.S.$9.1 billion in 1999, and it is clearly an expert in the design of seating systems. Lear's major competitors in the power seating business are Bertrand Pfaume (France), Mariner Corporation (originally Rockwell International), and the Johnson Controls Corporation. Since 1990, four major competitors have left the power seating business. These former competitors are Magna Corporation, Excel Corporation, Thompson Tennessee, and the Dura Corporation. The seat and seat component business is highly competitive worldwide.

HISTORY OF THE FACILITY

Elsie, Michigan, is a town of 700 people, located about 28 miles northeast of Lansing and about 110 miles northwest of Detroit, the major industrial area in the state. It is a farming community with a focus on dairy production and beef cattle. The Lear plant is the only major manufacturing employer in this town.

The plant opened in 1966 and was privately owned. During the 1966–1972 period, it made door latches, hood latches, and manual seat adjusters. The plant was sold to International Telephone and Telegraph (ITT) Automotive in 1973. ITT, which eventually became a division of United Technologies, aggressively pursued power seat assembly and power window regulator business. In the mid 1990s, ITT reconceptualized its business strategies to focus on rate of return and broke up its automotive group. Lear purchased the plant in 1997.

Lear's business strategy was and is to earn an acceptable rate of return while maximizing its share in the market for vehicle interiors. Local 1660 of the UAW represented the employees through all of these ownership changes and had to work through the necessary transitions. Financial results from the first quarter of 1999 indicate that this strategy has been successful for Lear, as the company increased earnings by 6.3 percent compared with the first quarter of 1999.

This Lear–Elsie plant currently manufactures power seat track assemblies, seat frames, torsion bars, and seat recliner mechanisms. Customers include Ford, General Motors, Daimler Chrysler, Saturn, and Toyota. The power seat track assemblies must be assembled to meet high customer standards. Because the driver's and passenger's seats are fitted onto these power seat tracks, any squeaks, noise, or wobble in their operation is likely to be immediately noticed by customers as a defect. The plant also has a repair shop capable of repairing seat track assemblies damaged in accidents or returned for other reasons.

The Lear–Elsie plant currently employs about 500 unionized production employees called process specialists, 15 skilled trades employees, 15 unit advisors (formerly supervisors), 8–10 clerical people, and about 8 material analysts and quality analysts in addition to the upper tier of managers. Employment levels have varied widely, though. In 1991, the plant employed 305 assembly employees. By 1995, the product market for sport utility vehicles had boosted the plant labor force to over 800 employees. In 1996, the bubble burst and jobs at Elsie fell from 800 to 258, as ITT management pulled all its Chrysler work from this plant and sent it to a sister ITT plant in Walker, Michigan, near Grand Rapids. Another sister plant in St. Thomas, Ontario (Canada), that did the same work as Lear–Elsie closed in 1996 due to high labor costs. Elsie realized that it had an opportunity to become more competitive by the mid 1990s, but it needed to find a way to survive.

An additional factor in understanding this plant is the turnover in the plant manager position. David Chambers, the current plant manager since 1996, was also plant manager from 1979 to 1987. Other plant managers served from 1987 to 1991 and from 1991 until 1996, while Chambers' career took him to roles as operations manager for five ITT plants and then as advanced engineering manager for ITT. He chose to return to the Elsie plant in 1996 and was retained by Lear when that company completed its purchase in 1997.

HISTORY AND BACKGROUND OF COLLECTIVE BARGAINING AT LEAR–ELSIE

Today, approximately 500 workers are represented by UAW Local 1660. The union was formed as Local 1660 in 1969 and has never merged or been amalgamated since then. There was one strike in 1979 that lasted for about 10 days over pension benefits. Use of third parties for arbitration is rare—possibly three or four cases in the last 30 years.

The union–management relationship with ITT was seen as "arm's length" at best and adversarial most of the time. The company saw all issues in terms of their business objectives. The union described this relationship as "take, take, take" in terms of ITT behavior, and it focused on filing grievances with little sense of any "give and take" in the process.

The 1997 negotiations began with ITT amid a flurry of rumors that the plant would be sold or closed. With three other ITT plants vying for seat track work, the union felt that the company held the upper hand in bargaining. The union had observed ITT changing its focus on automotive work from aggressive pursuit of business to letting workers and engineers be laid off. The workforce hoped for a new owner who would keep the Elsie plant open. Lear Corporation bought the plant and completed the negotiation process in 1997.

Lear Corporation differed from ITT in its stance toward unions. It pledged neutrality and recognized a union that possesses 51 percent of potential member cards stating a willingness to join that union. Furthermore, Lear has stated publicly that it "liked the UAW," and it enjoyed a good relationship with the international union. The parties have characterized their relationship since 1997 as "cooperative and collaborative."

COMPETITIVE PRESSURES

Employment in motor vehicle parts and accessories experienced growth in the last two decades of the 1980s. The trend of employment in the industry is presented in Figure 7.1. After a drop in the early 1980s, associated with the recession, employment in the industry began to grow in 1983 and continued to grow through 2000. Over the 20-year period, total employment increased by 57.5 percent, from approximately 349,500 to approximately 553,000. The growth rate in production employment was slightly greater; production employment grew by 60.5 percent, from 268,800 to 431,300.

But this overall growth in employment presented only an opportunity for the Elsie plant. There was no guarantee that all plants in the industry would share equally in this growth, or share at all. More specifically, given the small number of purchasers of motor vehicle parts and accessories, and the large contracts associated with those purchases, a small, stand-alone plant like Lear–Elsie found itself in a continual cycle of high risk, high reward; acquisition of a large contract meant increased employment; loss of a large contract meant a decline in employment.

Figure 7.1 Motor Vehicle Parts and Accessories, Total Employment and Production Employment in the United States, 1980–2000

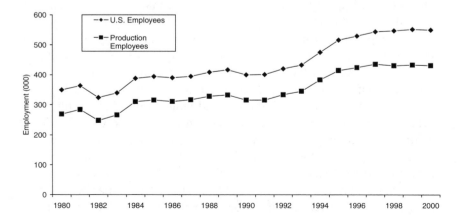

At the same time, global competition hit the Elsie plant in 1990–1991. Orders appeared from Toyota and Nissan, and suddenly employees realized that they were no longer linked only to domestic automotive production. At about the same time, Ford pulled its valuable Taurus contract from Elsie and gave it to Johnson Controls. Employees were shocked to see several lines closed. Since the plant is set up with decoupled assembly lines for each contract, employees can easily discern exactly which contracts the plant is gaining or losing. Employees no longer assumed that management or "someone" would always keep the Elsie plant supplied with work. Seeing employment drop from the 800s to the 200s in 1995 and 1996 ("high risk, high reward") demonstrated the vulnerability of this plant, as did the closing of the St. Thomas plant in Canada, and ITT's decision to move Chrysler work to the Walker plant.

COLLECTIVE BARGAINING, COMPETITIVENESS, AND EMPLOYMENT PROTECTION/CREATION: CONTRACT CHANGES

As noted, by the early 1990s the union at Elsie had become aware of the importance of competition and employment protection/creation at Elsie. These were also concerns of Lear when it assumed ownership of the plant. Of this joint concern, almost nothing was reflected in the formal collective bargaining agreement. Plant management stated that it could never guarantee levels of employment or offer job security. Job security was "based on seniority as long as the plant stays open." Job security was also seen as derived from "competitiveness and continuous improvement" in the 1997 collective bargaining agreement. This provision emphasizes a mutual commitment to team-based work systems, customer satisfaction, training and education for all employees, creation of a climate of mutual dignity and respect, and use of participation to improve productivity, efficiency, quality, and cost performance. The provision also states that employees will assume personal responsibility and accountability for the Elsie plant's success.

A major gain for Lear in the 1997 contract was the ability to collapse six job classifications into one to gain flexibility. The union feels that merging assembly, maintenance, material handling, inspection, forklift, and salvage employees into one classification overdoes the flexibility concept and should be rethought on the next negotiation.

Lear management's vision was comprehensive. It downloaded quality, scrap, and cost objectives for each line to employee teams. It changed the designation of supervisor to unit advisor and demanded that they assume a teaching, coaching, and facilitating role with employee teams rather than a directive role. A 1999 assessment is that some supervisors still complain about their loss of power to direct employees, but that this role transition has been mostly successful except for periodic incidents of old ways of thinking. The philosophy is that "we are all in this together," and that everyone needs to work together to improve multiskilled and multifunctioning employees.

Combined with the collapsing of six classifications into one, the plant has gained huge cost efficiencies. The Elsie collective bargaining agreement differs from most other Lear plants in that it does not specify production standards. Elsie management believes people in teams working in units can do a better job of setting and achieving competitive standards than by using a top-down industrial engineering approach.

The parties did not limit themselves to competitiveness in the 1997 negotiations. A lump sum payment of $750 was provided to each employee. In addition, the parties incorporated a "neutrality pledge" to accept the union as a partner at Lear workplaces.

FORMAL NONCONTRACTUAL MECHANISMS

The current philosophy is anchored in a formal noncontractual participation system. The company and union created a joint steering team (JST) that reports to a planning team consisting of the plant manager, plant superintendent, union president, and bargaining chair of Local 1660. The JST is a parallel organization that bridges upper leadership to the workforce. The JST includes the plant manager, plant superintendent, human resources manager, quality manager, materials manager, and quality analyst. Their union counterparts on the JST are the president, bargaining chair, and volunteers such as the statistical process control coordinator (SPC) and a process specialist employee from the shop floor. The JST charters four design and development committees to serve all 14 business unit teams on the line. Design and development function teams are staffed by at least one JST member plus technical volunteers. Four teams are used: finance, people and groups, equipment and facilities, and information. These teams act as in-house consultants to help each business unit (assembly teams) with budgets, layout, process improvements, and team issues necessary to remain competitive and attract new business. All design and development team projects lead to recommendations to the JST. The JST may also create ad hoc teams to host recognition dinners, examine rewards, or to be a community service team to help the plant support its community. These JST mechanisms have created formal opportunities for employees to become engaged in making their business units more productive and customer responsive.

The plant now runs as an open book and "glass wall" plant with all cost, quality, scrap, and productivity data made available to employees in business units. Management still reserves the right to allocate employees across business units.

Both union and management stressed the need for training. Plant employees indicated that they had attended courses in SPC, pull training, traceability, process analysis, QS 9000, team interaction training, compass, and problem solving. Training may be initiated by either management or the union; the business unit makes the decision. Both management and the union see the current system as effective in promoting competitiveness and in creating and protecting jobs. Other formal but noncontractual elements of the current situation include the 40 hours guarantee, which allows employees to volunteer to work extra hours elsewhere in the plant or just take time off if a line runs short of materials or work during any week, and the "six pack" system, where each business unit works on the top six line problems and issues reported each week. The JST system is clearly evolving to meet jointly perceived needs for competitiveness and job protection/creation.

CREATING A FORMAL, NONCONTRACTUAL PARTICIPATION SYSTEM

ITT had experimented with teams since the mid 1980s and had focused on individual skill training. Team roll-outs failed twice. But plant management and the union learned together how to build a successful participation system. They read books on teams, worked with private consultants, and jointly benchmarked firms such as Johnsonville Sausage, Sealed Power, Saturn, and Delphi-Saginaw, firms known for having successfully installed team-based work systems. Company and union leadership attended seminars on team development offered at North Texas State University. New union leadership and the return of David Chambers as plant manager were seen as plusses in terms of consistent leadership of this competitive effort. The plant experimented with new work system concepts until it reached a workable solution for the Elsie work context.

COMPETITION AND EMPLOYMENT PROTECTION/ CREATION WITHIN DIFFERING MANUFACTURING PARADIGMS

The Elsie plant of the Lear Corporation and Local 1660 of the UAW have had to bargain competitiveness, employment security, and growth issues in the context of major changes in the manufacturing systems of the plant. These three manufacturing systems or paradigms are those of: 1) mass production (Womack, Jones, and Roos 1990); 2) sociotechnical systems production (Trist and Bamforth 1951; Niepce and Molleman 1998); and 3) lean manufacturing (Ohno 1988; Kenney and Florida 1993; Womack and Jones 1996). Each system differs in fundamental dimensions from the others. These manufacturing systems will be discussed in turn and related to the business context and the collective bargaining relationship at the Elsie plant.

MASS PRODUCTION AT LEAR–ELSIE

Mass production is based upon the ability of a system to standardize outputs from a manufacturing or service process. It is an American system that spread around the world from 1915 to the present, and until the late 1980s, received few challenges from competing systems. Mass production is based on the principle of economies of scale. Its components include functional specialization, infrequent job rotation, tightly supervised machine-paced work, many job classifications, and problem solving by manufacturing and staff (engineering, accounting, production control, labor relations, quality, and human resources, to name a few). It also utilizes a deskilled workforce, work standards imposed on workers, seniority as the basis for wages and promotion, arm's-length relationships with suppliers, and adversarial labor relations. The general objective of mass production was creation of products of "good enough" quality and to maintain large inventories as buffers against machine or worker problems. While mass production can be employed with management styles ranging from coercive to enlightened, it still represents a problematic manufacturing model in the twenty-first century.

The Lear–Elsie plant was run by several owners as a mass production facility until the mid 1990s. Management was in control of the plant, and workers received little training, did not work in teams, received little information about quality, and were tightly supervised. Employment at the Elsie plant fluctuated wildly as it competed with other plants to be awarded lines of business. While unionized since 1969, the relationship was characterized by company "take-away's" according to the union. The basic hope of the union was that a more enlightened owner would purchase the plant. When the Lear Corporation purchased the plant in 1997, it brought a new manufacturing paradigm plus a plant manager who knew and respected the plant and its people. The new manufacturing paradigm of team-based work systems closely followed the sociotechnical systems model.

SOCIOTECHNICAL TEAM-BASED SYSTEMS AT LEAR–ELSIE

The team-based "sociotechnical" systems (STS) bargained in the 1997 contract by plant manager David Chambers were American but were built heavily on ideas first tested in England (Trist and Bamforth 1951) and northern Europe (Berggren 1992). These systems were designed to create high levels of worker satisfaction, which was believed to lead to high levels of quality production and retention of workers. These STS approaches grouped employees into large teams, changed the role of supervisor into more of a group facilitator, incorporated team process skills and quality skills into the training of all group members, and led to frequent team meetings to discuss plant performance—the "glass wall" concept. The union was accepted by management as a partner rather than an adversary, and its opinion was sought on all workplace changes. Ergonomics received new attention, and workers were given more freedom to design and schedule tasks as long as quality standards and productivity standards were met. Employees were urged to deeply identify with their team and the product it produced for each of the contracts in the plant.

This STS story is largely the story told in this case, which portrays the successful shift to a team-based work system; improved worker, management, and union attitudes; a successful contract negotiation in 1997; and the general prosperity of the plant. The team-based system was seen by all as incorporating the elements necessary to maintain a competitive posture and to secure jobs for the Elsie plant for the foreseeable future. The case ended with appreciation for the versatility of the collective bargaining process and noncontractual arrangements in securing a positive future for the Elsie plant, its union, and its workforce. However, in a surprising turn of events, an interview conducted in 2001 indicated that the plant had largely discarded this paradigm and had shifted to lean manufacturing in 2000, thus removing many team-based elements from the contract bargained by Lear and UAW Local 1660.

LEAN MANUFACTURING AT LEAR–ELSIE

The lean manufacturing system originated in Asia as the Toyota Production System created by Taiichi Ohno (1988). Lean manufacturing became known to the West when popularized by the International Motor Vehicle Program at MIT. The book *The Machine That Changed the World* (Womack, Jones, and Roos 1990) startled U.S. and European mass producers by showing that lean principles allow factories to operate with half the space of comparable mass production facilities. Further, lean plants showed only half the defects found in mass products, used half the hours of human effort, needed only one-tenth the amount of in-process inventory, and reduced product development times by one-third. The best European STS plants were shown to be nearly one-third less efficient than lean plants in Japan and those of Japanese transplants in the United States. Controversy arose immediately as intellectuals of the STS orientation (Berggren 1992; Van Eijnatten, Hoevenaars, and Rutte 1992; Fucini and Fucini 1990; Parker and Slaughter 1995) launched attacks on lean manufacturing as simply being an advanced form of "Fordism." Lean advocates (Adler and Cole 1993) responded that lean plants could not only out-produce other paradigms, but that the secret of the lean approach was in its superior way of promoting organizational learning through its standardized work systems and team-based suggestion systems. This is the direction taken by the Elsie plant in 2000.

The lean system at Lear–Elsie is a close fit with lean principles (Ohno 1988). Chambers felt that the STS-type large teams had become too independent and rigid. They set up boundaries and isolated themselves from other plant teams. Their working autonomy was not translated into sharing ideas to help the plant but instead to become more impervious to ideas from others in the plant. These comments echo the Adler and Cole (1993) comments about the downsides of the STS team systems. In contrast, lean teams are small and are led by team leaders; they are not "semi-autonomous" but are tightly linked to other teams on their line. Lean is characterized by "andon" systems (which allow workers to stop the line in the event of materials shortage or quality problem), standardized work, just-in-time inventory and material handling systems, quick team meetings, and a focus on eliminating waste.

"Kaizen" (continuous improvement) events are used for extensive process and quality assessment of specific target areas in the plant. All of these systems and processes have been installed at the Lear–Elsie plant since 2000. The union allowed the company to remove many of the team concepts and install lean principles in order to support management's goal of keeping the facility competitive. According to Chambers, the UAW Local 1660 leaders were somewhat cynical that lean production was simply a new "flavor of the month," but they had built up enough trust in management after the 1997 contract to be willing to negotiate a shift to lean manufacturing. The union felt that both approaches are team-based and that team concepts were supported by the membership.

The lean system is already producing successes for the Elsie plant. Plant in-process inventory has dropped 22 percent. Four kaizen events have been held. Employees are contributing a steady flow of suggestions. "Glass-wall" knowledge of plant functioning is still shared with all employees. Employees have been trained in the seven types of waste and how to use the "5's" model of workplace organization. Cross-functional teams are extensively used to solve problems and ensure the sharing of best practices and ideas. The Elsie plant has successfully launched new product lines and has reached productivity and quality performance levels faster than ever before. Plant employment levels have been maintained. The plant's layout and footprint are the current constraints to future growth, but upcoming kaizen events are seen as likely to create improved space utilization so new product lines can be attracted to the plant. By having the courage to use the collective bargaining process to make a successful team-based plant even better, the union and the company have exemplified the creativity and flexibility necessary to keep a small auto supplier plant economically competitive and able to sustain employment levels in a small rural community.

CONCLUSION

In an industry with growing employment overall, but with the possibility of unstable employment at any single facility, competitiveness means appropriating for that plant a share of the overall industry employment gains. In 1999 and in 2001, this plant was working at capacity with new jobs scheduled to replace jobs that will be closed out due to decisions made about the product's life cycle by automotive manufacturers. Both management and union report that most employees are happy with the plant today and are pleased with its competitive position and its future likelihood of job protection and creation. Management spokespersons see a complete turnaround by both sides. Ten years ago, employee complaints were met with the statement "go write a grievance." Five years ago, management would take the time to argue but would still resolve matters by telling the union to "go write a grievance." Today the situation is characterized as both sides being willing to admit it if they are wrong. Plus, both sides are likely to give each other some leeway because trust has been established. Management recognizes it is always fighting inertia and resistance to change from both supervisors/unit advisors and employees. Union reservations to agree to total success of this system stem from the company's use of bargaining power in the 1997 negotiation and the resulting classification collapse. The union believes the process of getting competitive could have been handled better.

Management and union seem to agree that sharing information makes everyone hungry to learn even more about the business and to become multiskilled and even more knowledgeable about the competitive global environment. Both are also likely to believe that Elsie was fortunate to have Chambers return as plant manager and point to his engineering background, product knowledge, benchmarking experience in Europe, Japan, and the United States, plus his vision and people skills. He earns approval by his willingness to aggressively pursue business for Lear–Elsie.

Finally, both union and management express appreciation for the institution of collective bargaining as a way to forge new relationships and to create new participation mechanisms necessary to foster competition and to protect and create jobs in response to global competitive pressures. The Elsie plant's ability to illustrate the worldwide search for an optimum manufacturing paradigm while fully utilizing collective bargaining and noncontractual mechanisms makes this an important case study. This small North American plant exemplifies the global search for methods of achieving competitiveness while maintaining employment levels. In that sense, the Lear plant in Elsie represents a prototypical example of a unionized facility attempting to maintain employment in the United States.

Note

The authors would like to thank the interviewees cited in the chapter.

Unless otherwise noted parenthetically in the text, the material in this chapter is based on Chambers and Laxton (1999), Rathbun and Tyler (1999), Jordan and Klatt (1999), Jablowski (1999), and Chambers (2001).

References

Adler, Paul, and Robert Cole. 1993. "Designed for Learning: A Tale of Two Auto Plants." *Sloan Management Review* 34(3): 85–94.

Berggren, C. 1992. *Alternatives to Lean Production: Work Organization in the Swedish Auto Industry.* Ithaca, New York: ILR Press.

Chambers, David. Lear–Elsie interview, October 3, 2001.

Chambers, David, and Julie Laxton. Lear–Elsie interview, February 25, 1999.

Fucini, Joseph, and Susan Fucini. 1990. *Working for the Japanese: Inside Mazda's American Auto Plant.* New York: Free Press, Macmillan.

Jablowski, Stan. Lear–Elsie interview, February 25, 1999.

Jordan, Christopher, and Terry Klatt. Lear–Elsie interview, February 25, 1999.

Kenney, M., and Richard Florida. 1993. *Beyond Mass Production: The Japanese System and Its Transfer to the U.S.* New York: Oxford University Press.

Niepce, W., and E. Molleman. 1998. "Work Design Issues in Lean Production from a Sociotechnical Systems Perspective." *Human Relations* 51(3): 259–287.

Ohno, T. 1988. *Toyota Production System: Beyond Large-Scale Production.* Cambridge, Massachusetts: Productivity Press.

Parker, Mike, and Jane Slaughter. 1995. "Unions and Management by Stress." In *Lean Work: Empowerment and Exploitation in the Global Auto Industry,* Steve Babson, ed. Detroit: Wayne State University Press.

Rathbun, Linda, and Jack Tyler. UAW Local 1660 joint interview, February 25, 1999.

Trist, E.L., and K. Bamforth. 1951. "Some Social and Psychological Consequences of Longwall Coal Mining." *Human Relations* 4(1): 3–38.

Van Eijnatten, F.M., A.M. Hoevenaars, and C.G. Rutte. 1992. "Holistic and Participative (Re)design; Contemporary STSD Modeling in the Netherlands." In *Organizational Change and Innovation: Psychological Perspectives and Practices in Europe*, Dian M. Hosking and N. Anderson, eds. London: Routledge, pp. 183–207.

Womack, J.P., and D. Jones. 1996. *Lean Thinking: Banish Waste and Create Wealth in Your Corporation*. New York: Simon and Schuster.

Womack, J.P., D.T. Jones, and D. Roos. 1990. *The Machine That Changed the World*. New York: Macmillan.

8
Health Care

Sparrow Health System, Lansing, Michigan, and Professional Employees Council of Sparrow Hospital/Michigan Nurses Association

Michael J. Polzin
Peter Berg
Michigan State University

Employment in the hospital industry continues to increase despite major financial challenges confronting the industry. Expenses in U.S. hospitals doubled over the decade 1986–1996, and these costs are expected to grow at a rate of about 6.5 percent annually (Strunk, Ginsburg, and Gabel 2001). The rapidly rising costs are driving hospitals to exact tough measures to control expenses, including mergers, acquisitions, and closures. Consolidation has reduced the number of hospitals by more than 10 percent, from 6,841 in 1986 to 6,201 in 1996 (Plunkett 2000). However, employment levels in hospitals have not changed correspondingly, with employment in hospitals increasing by more than 500,000 over the level (4.28 million) of the prior decade (Plunkett 2000). Thus, collective bargaining in hospitals occurs within an environment quite different from that experienced by unionized manufacturers, who often are confronted with excess capacity within their industries and shrinking workforce needs.

This case focuses on Sparrow Hospital in Lansing, Michigan. The chapter identifies many of the changes that confronted the hospital over the past few years and examines how the collective bargaining relationship affected the way union and management responded to those changes.

DESCRIPTION OF THE BUSINESS

Sparrow Health System is a nonprofit, community-governed, comprehensive, integrated health delivery and financing system headquartered in Lansing, Michigan. At the heart of the Sparrow Health System is Sparrow Hospital, a 502-bed regional, acute-care facility, and another hospital, the St. Lawrence campus, a formerly independent hospital. Nurses and other professional employees of the health system are represented by the Professional Employees Council of Sparrow Hospital (PECSH), which is affiliated with the Michigan Nurses Association (MNA), an affiliate of the American Nurses Association. Sparrow owns and operates a nursing home in the Lansing area as well as over 30 health-related facilities such as clinics, physician practices, and laboratory draw stations.

The delivery of health care services is in major transition, as third-party payers (insurance companies, state government, and federal Medicare programs) are demanding reduced—or at least contained—costs, while patients are demanding improved quality, greater accessibility of services or resources, and higher degrees of satisfaction. The industry as a whole is being affected profoundly, and the impact on Sparrow is no exception.

Employment in the health care industry is in the midst of a long-term secular increase. Figure 8.1 shows the trend in health services employment in the Lansing metropolitan area from 1988 to 2000, and Figure 8.2 shows the trend for health services employment nationally. As seen in these figures, both are increasing. Lansing area health care employment increased from about 12,000 to 16,600 between 1988 and 2000, a jump of roughly 38.3 percent. National health care employment during this same period increased from approximately 7.1 million to 10.1 million, an increase of 42.1 percent.

HISTORY OF SPARROW HEALTH SYSTEM

Lansing, the capital of Michigan, is a medium-sized city with a 1996 population of approximately 129,000 (U.S. Bureau of the Census

Figure 8.1 Health Services Employment in Lansing–East Lansing, Michigan, 1988–2000

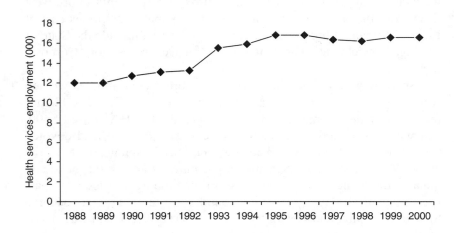

Figure 8.2 Health Services Employment in the United States, 1988–2000

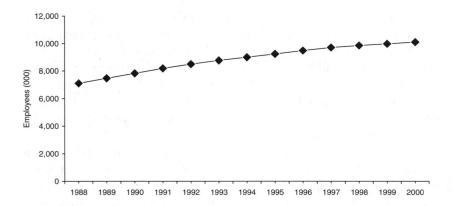

1996a) in the midst of a metropolitan area with a 1996 population of approximately 450,000 (U.S. Bureau of the Census 1996b). The city is located in southern lower Michigan, approximately 90 miles northwest of Detroit, the state's largest city, and approximately 90 miles east of Lake Michigan. Other major employers in the area include the State of Michigan, Michigan State University, and General Motors Corporation.

Sparrow was founded in 1896 by a group of civic-minded women who came together to form a community hospital. The 114 charter members of the Women's Hospital Association (WHA) raised $400, and with that rented a house, hired a doctor and nurse, and devoted their time and resources to keeping their tiny hospital afloat. In the early 1900s, Edward W. Sparrow, a prominent Lansing businessman, donated the money and property that formed the base of today's Sparrow Hospital. Today, the hospital founded by the WHA has become Sparrow Hospital and Health System and serves the health care needs of more than 120,000 people annually.

HISTORY AND BACKGROUND OF COLLECTIVE BARGAINING AT SPARROW HEALTH SYSTEM

Sparrow Health System employs approximately 5,600 people, of which 1,630 are members of PECSH. The bargaining unit is comprised of all registered nurses and other health care professionals (pharmacists, medical technicians, physical therapists, occupational therapists, dietitians, social workers, and mental health therapists) who are employed by Sparrow Hospital. Members of the bargaining unit may be found working in both of the hospital campuses, as well as in other health system affiliates.

The bargaining unit was first organized in 1988 in response to an increasing number of unilateral decisions by management, particularly with respect to changing work schedules and shifting assignments. Employment trends at Sparrow over the last decade were difficult to determine, as during that time, Sparrow, like many other health care organizations, merged with another hospital (in Lansing) and added many ancillary services, such as laboratories and outpatient facilities.

The collective bargaining relationship began as traditionally adversarial. Contract negotiations in 1991 were very difficult, and a mediator from the U.S. Federal Mediation and Conciliation Service (FMCS) was called in to help reach an agreement. Similarly, in 1994, an FMCS mediator was also called in after a strike vote was taken. The issue at the center of the 1994 conflict was staffing, as many employees— nurses, in particular—were concerned for the well-being of patients. Despite its history of traditional adversarial bargaining, the labor–management relationship changed in 1993, when management began to consult more with union leadership on key decisions that would have an impact on bargaining unit members. These initial cooperative practices were well received, as both parties sensed that a new relationship was needed.

In late 1994, PECSH and Sparrow management, with the assistance of a third party from Michigan State University, met to consider developing a joint labor–management approach to redesigning patient care. The initial meeting had positive results. The parties found that their visions for what they wanted the union–management relationship to become were similar and consequently agreed to a set of principles that would guide their interactions with respect to the redesign process and other matters. Those principles then formed the basis for new provisions in the 1994 collective agreement that created a structure and articulated a purpose for a formal joint labor–management committee. This Mutual Gains Committee (MGC) became the forum through which decisions regarding workplace restructuring that directly affected employees would be made. The MGC ultimately took on a range of issues including staffing and contract interpretation.

COMPETITIVE PRESSURES CONFRONTING SPARROW HEALTH SYSTEM AND PECSH

Hospitals and the health care industry are under tremendous competitive pressures, but it is pressure of a fundamentally different kind than what manufacturing firms face. As noted, unlike manufacturing, employment in health care is increasing. Sparrow's competitive challenges are thus primarily related to the changing structure of the health

care industry: increased local competition from rival health care organizations, and pressure from third-party payers—insurance companies—to keep fees as low as possible. The increase in surgical centers
and clinics has increased competition for health care services and good
personnel. Insurance companies continue to pressure hospitals to
reduce costs. Moreover, recent reductions in federal Medicare reim-
bursements, which have resulted in lower payments to hospitals, have
added to the cost pressures on hospitals. Customer expectations are
driving demands for utilization of emerging technologies and resources
and greater satisfaction with respect to the patient and family experience. Sparrow Hospital began to experience these competitive pressures in the early 1990s, though they were not particularly unique to
Sparrow.

A major competitive pressure that was unique to Lansing, Michigan, if not to Sparrow, in the 1990s was the merger of two major hospitals in the city and, subsequently, the proposed buyout of that new
entity by a large, for-profit hospital chain (Columbia/HCA). That
would have led to the creation of one of the first for-profit hospitals in
the state. The buyout was ultimately unsuccessful after considerable
public outcry and intervention from the State's attorney general. Nonetheless, the consolidation of hospital services prior to the failed buyout
effort and the subsequent affiliation of the new merged hospital (and
now a much more significant competitor) with a health care system in
Flint, Michigan, prompted Sparrow to merge with St. Lawrence Hospital in 1997.

Competitive pressures, reductions in payments to hospitals, and
Columbia's attempt to enter the Lansing market prompted other
changes at Sparrow. For example, purchasing practices were examined. In some cases, nursing staff felt that they could no longer get the
supplies they wanted, only what was cheapest. Employees reported
feeling a loss of input and control. Patient–staff ratios increased. Nursing staff believed that some nonnursing personnel were doing tasks for
patients that traditionally had been handled by nurses, and they feared
that patient care might be compromised. Financial benchmarking practices also took hold to the degree that a number system was applied to
the severity of patient illness. This was consistent with what most hospitals were doing to address the lower payment issue. However, some
nursing staff were frustrated when the numeric indicators available

were not sufficient to justify dedication of resource levels to a patient. Some nurses feared that their ability to have input into prescribing the care needed for their patients would be eroded. Contentiousness around the contract reflected changes in these business practices.

Sparrow responded to the pressure to reduce costs by benchmarking its costs to other hospitals nationally. The benchmarks furthered the argument that costs at Sparrow needed to be brought in line with hospitals of similar size. Sparrow also responded by increasing nurse–patient ratios to standards in place in other high-performance hospitals. Sparrow also began to experience a shortage of nurses through an interesting twist of fate. A national nursing shortage and a very high patient census resulted in unintended consequences that even Sparrow's good intentions could not have foreseen. In order to have positions for all staff after the merger, Sparrow left dozens of vacant positions unfilled so that they would be able to make and keep a promise of no layoffs as a consequence of the merger. No one counted on the fact that a number of employees, mostly from the St. Lawrence facility, saw the merger as an opportunity to seek other employment. Because of the tight labor market, they found other employment rather easily, which left Sparrow with many positions unfilled.

COLLECTIVE BARGAINING, COMPETITIVENESS, AND EMPLOYMENT PROTECTION/CREATION

Changes in Contract Language

Management's proposal to introduce a patient care redesign initiative had a significant impact on collective bargaining and the union–management relationship at Sparrow. Management believed that patient care redesign would improve quality and perhaps even increase patient satisfaction by reducing the number of different employees involved in delivering care. Instead, all services would be delivered through patient-care teams. In 1992–1993, management brought in consultants to help redesign patient care using a model known as "patient-focused care." Initially, there was no union involvement in selecting consultants or in the process of exploring or designing the patient-care delivery system. Negative reaction was widespread throughout the Sparrow Health System. Management realized that there would be no acceptance of or commitment to a change this significant if employees were not involved in the effort. Consequently, PECSH leadership was asked to join management in overseeing the effort to redesign the patient-care delivery system. PECSH leadership entered the discussions with an expectation that union and management would work as equals, an idea readily accepted by management. This attitude was consistent with the belief (shared by Sparrow management and staff and PECSH/MNA leadership, and supported by Sparrow's CEO) that people should be involved in making decisions that affected them and their work. Consultants from Michigan State University facilitated an initial meeting between union and management leadership to explore the scope and boundaries of that work, as well as to begin to construct a framework upon which that work would be built. Their discussions resulted in a set of guiding principles that union and management leadership agreed would undergird their work together. The principles also formed the basis for the creation of a joint labor–management mutual gains committee that was negotiated as part of the 1994 collective agreement.

Formal Structures

Sparrow used the Mutual Gains Committee to create a structure and process for redesigning work around a patient-focused care model. The committee visited other organizations, read books, and benchmarked their practices against other hospitals as a way of developing their own model of work organization. The Sparrow model decentralizes some nonnursing services, such as phlebotomy and housekeeping, to the unit level. Typically, the redesigned unit forms teams led by registered nurses (RNs), who delegate responsibilities and monitor performance outcomes. The teams consist of patient care technicians (PCT) (formerly orderlies), who perform uncomplicated respiratory treatments and suctioning, phlebotomy, and EKGs (along with licensed practical nurses). Patient care assistants (PCA), formerly part of the centralized housekeeping staff, are also part of the team on the unit. The PCAs are responsible for cleaning the room, transportation, tray passing and setup, and assisting with beds and baths.

This redesigned work system that integrates functions is supposed to increase patient, physician, and employee satisfaction, as well as improve care and decrease expenses. The teams have yet to be widely implemented across units in the hospital, and their effects seem to be mixed. High patient volume and staff vacancies resulting in tight staffing levels seem to particularly undermine the patient-focused care model. Moreover, the lack of RN training in delegation skills (although various leadership development training sessions were provided) and some RNs' unwillingness to accept authority—and some middle managers' reluctance to give it up—have hindered the implementation of work redesign.

A national nursing shortage, as well as shortages of other key occupations, put pressure on the ability of Sparrow staff to address patient needs and enhance patient satisfaction. This also contributes to additional overtime and recruitment costs and recruitment and retention problems. Indeed, the experience at Sparrow strongly suggests that the success of the patient care redesign is predicated on having sufficient staffing levels. Sparrow and PECSH decided, through the Mutual Gains Committee, to address the shortages jointly. A joint labor–management committee was established to address recruitment and retention of nurses, pharmacists, and other occupations where there is the greatest need. At the same time, the parties maintain their commitment to having sufficient staff coverage at all times. Again, through the Mutual Gains Committee, the parties developed minimal acceptable staffing levels for all units. When staffing falls below the minimal level, a joint committee awards $200 to the employees in the affected unit, whose responsibility it is to cover the absent or unscheduled employees. The employees in the unit are free to do what they wish with the funds.

When the merger occurred, all nurses and professional health care employees from St. Lawrence were brought in to PECSH in such a way that the St. Lawrence seniority became the seniority within the entire bargaining unit. This was done because management and PECSH believed this was the fair thing to do for the St. Lawrence staff, to build support for the merger and make the new members feel welcome in PECSH. Nonetheless, there was a wage differential between many of the Sparrow employees and the St. Lawrence employees, due in part to the difference in financial performance of Sparrow and St. Lawrence.

Union and management negotiated a one-time, lump-sum bonus to be paid to Sparrow employees, in lieu of a wage increase, so as not to exacerbate the differential. PECSH and Sparrow also negotiated into the 1998 agreement a performance-based, add-on gain-sharing plan. Payout is based on achieving targeted hospital performance.

Informal Actions and Programs

The work redesign efforts have spun off informal applications of the patient care model. In at least one department, the manager and employees are using a participatory process to make changes. Though there has been no formal redesign of that department yet, there is a continual focus on management and staff working together to make operational improvements.

Conversations between PECSH and Sparrow prior to the merger went far to strengthen their relationship, which helped to maintain a positive community image during that period. Management kept the union informed throughout the process and agreed early on to incorporate St. Lawrence professional staff into the PECSH bargaining unit. That led to PECSH working to develop strategies to welcome and integrate new staff into the Sparrow system. On the matter of the potential entry of Columbia/HCA into the Lansing market, PECSH gave definitive support to Sparrow at public hearings to add to the case against entry of the for-profit chain into the local health care market. Other actions enhanced the strength of the labor–management relationship, which is significant in helping Sparrow respond to external competition. During a recent "Nurses Week," PECSH and Sparrow management joined forces in erecting a billboard that combined both a nurses theme and a collaboration theme. For the past several years, Sparrow management has funded several PECSH officers to attend a national conference on "Unions and Health Care." Prior to the merger, both Sparrow and PECSH leadership presented ideas on joint labor–management cooperation to representatives of the Mercy Health Care System, the parent company of St. Lawrence. Both parties were pleased to work together in support of the merger. Their cooperation helped facilitate completion of the negotiations and approval process.

The collective bargaining process itself was affected by the positive experience of working within the Mutual Gains Committee structure. In the 1998 negotiations, the parties decided to incorporate an explicit interest-based bargaining approach and brought in a third party that was skilled in using this type of model. The consultant taught the bargaining committees how to use the model through a formal education program and then facilitated the bargaining process. An agreement that was satisfactory to all was reached, albeit in the last week of negotiations; when compensation was on the table, bargaining reverted to the much more traditional distributive style. Contract administration has also been affected positively by the cooperative efforts of the parties. There are sincere attempts to settle grievances outside the formal grievance process. In prior years, many managers were trained in non-traditional problem-solving practices. Due to turnover in management and union leadership, the parties recognize a need to recommit time to ensure that problem-solving occurs in a manner consistent with the mutual gains approach.

OBSERVATIONS AND CONCLUSIONS

Though the mutual gains process has had a significant and positive influence on the Sparrow Health System, the impact has been felt most by those in leadership positions. Some union leaders think the process is not as visible to many rank-and-file members. Others have difficulty separating the mutual gains or joint labor–management approach to problem solving or change from the patient-care redesign process itself. For those who have not been involved in work redesign—and that would still be the majority of employees at Sparrow—the only opportunity they would have to see applications of the mutual gains process would be through the day-to-day interactions within their respective departments. Both union and management leadership acknowledge that most middle managers have yet to be trained in interest-based methods and techniques to apply to problems or conflicts that arise. PECSH and Sparrow management have tried to make educating mid- and first-level managers in the basics of the mutual gains or interest-based process a priority, but the competitive pressures that Sparrow has had to face in the past few years have taken a great deal of attention and diverted resources away from diffusing the mutual gains process throughout the hospital.

For Sparrow Health System, the collective bargaining structure and process has had a positive impact on factors related to competitiveness primarily through the mutual gains provisions in the agreement. The mutual gains process gave all employees, both union and nonunion, a voice and a vote in the patient care redesign effort. Indeed, before a redesign is implemented in a unit, it must receive at least a majority vote from all employees in the unit. The mutual gains process has also helped improve problem solving within departments, particularly problems that might otherwise end up as grievances. More managers are likely to support problem solving at the lowest level, and this concept is strongly supported by the human resources department. Over time, many managers have come to a different appreciation of PECSH/MNA and no longer see it as a threat, but rather as a partner in the delivery of high-quality health care. Many rank-and-file members, once they see that management is approachable, go directly to their supervisors to work out problems. Nonetheless, both parties acknowledge that they need to reinvest time and energy in their relationship.

The relationship that PECSH and Sparrow management developed as a consequence of mutual gains has also helped address the threat from external competitors. PECSH and management spoke as a team against the proposed entry of the for-profit Columbia/HCA into the community-based Lansing health care market. PECSH leadership also played a significant role in building acceptance for the merger with St. Lawrence among its own members as well as among the affected workers from St. Lawrence. In addition, PECSH took clear steps to try to integrate St. Lawrence workers into the Sparrow system and to reduce wage differentials that could adversely affect employee morale and turnover rates. Through the Mutual Gains Committee, a committee on recruitment and retention has met several times in an attempt to reduce the shortage of nursing and other personnel, which adversely affects patient care as well as cost of care, two measurements that are important to evaluating the success of redesign efforts.

The degree of job retention and creation that can be attributed to the collective bargaining structure and process at Sparrow is more difficult to assess. PECSH has only been in existence for about 11 years. During that time, some services have expanded and some have contracted. Certainly, the merger with St. Lawrence resulted in a net gain in jobs for the system as a whole, but with the serious nursing and professional staff shortages that exist nationwide, many of those jobs remain unfilled. It is true that some St. Lawrence employees did not make the move to Sparrow when offered the opportunity and took other employment instead, both with other area health care employers as well as outside the health care field entirely. But it does not appear to be the case that these employment choices had much to do with the unionized status of Sparrow Health System. Rather, they seemed to be based on various other factors such as personal preferences, high patient volumes at Sparrow atypical of those at St. Lawrence, high patient acuity, higher starting wages in some cases, and a desire for a different workload than that anticipated at Sparrow.

Job retention is taken very seriously at Sparrow, and the collective agreement and the positive labor–management relations here provided incentive to Sparrow to strengthen job retention practices. Sparrow management learned several years ago when first exploring patient care redesign that the only way they would get the acceptance, if not the cooperation, of nursing and professional staff was to involve them in designing and implementing the changes. Along with that, they also acknowledged that to reduce fears about dislocation, they must address issues of employment security. Management has a standing verbal agreement with PECSH that no person would lose employment with Sparrow Health System as a result of job redesign.

Issues remain, however, that will require additional attention from PECSH and Sparrow management as they continue their efforts to retain or increase their competitive standing. Patient care redesign efforts have affected only a small portion of Sparrow departments and employees. The amount of time needed to redesign patient care systems in a unit was grossly underestimated. Many nurses claim that they do not feel empowered to make decisions, even though there is contractual language to support them. Many managers have not been exposed to the concepts of mutual gains and interest-based approaches to problem solving, so there is disparity in the ways in which people address problems and grievances. In some units, turnover rates are fairly high—not necessarily higher than industry averages, but still high enough to strain staffing levels. The gains achieved by units that have been redesigned are not all that conclusive. Costs are up (perhaps as a consequence of staffing shortages), while quality indicators, such as infection control and patient satisfaction, are improved. Staff often report, however, that their satisfaction is mixed. Sparrow has long practiced what is known as primary nursing—essentially because Sparrow employed no aides; nurses did everything, affording them the opportunity to develop strong and satisfying relationships with patients. Typically, patient care redesign changes this situation so that the role of the staff nurse is different. For some, this lessens the opportunity to develop strong and satisfying relationships with patients.

Changes in reimbursement patterns from public and private payers continue to drive changes in Sparrow to a degree that significantly controls choices that are made and how work gets done. The amount of paperwork has been increasing profoundly, which results in managers and staff increasing their workload without having additional impact on operations. The excess demands on managers mean that they have less time to look at fundamental changes that would improve work. This leads to managers leaving their jobs because of the perceived loss of impact.

Wage differentials between Sparrow and St. Lawrence employees continue to exist and fester, despite mechanisms in place from the 1998 negotiations to reduce such inequalities. Reports of people working side by side doing the same job yet receiving different salaries are commonplace. The merger with St. Lawrence added many issues to Sparrow's mix and they will likely require attention for some time.

PECSH/MNA and Sparrow management can point to much progress since mutual gains provisions were included in the 1994 collective agreement. These improvements followed from intentional changes in attitudes and degree of support from management and PECSH/MNA leadership toward an improved working relationship in the preceding two years. If all of the competitive issues have not been effectively addressed, then at least the Mutual Gains Committee and the resulting cooperative labor–management process provides a forum with which to address them. The health care industry will continue to offer challenges to organizations like Sparrow as it continues to develop growth strategies in an industry dominated by fewer but larger organizations competing to provide a range of health services, such as outpatient and laboratory services rather than simply inpatient health care. The cooperative labor–management mechanisms that PECSH/

MNA and Sparrow have forged through their collective bargaining process are likely to serve them well as they continue to provide high-quality service to the residents of mid Michigan.

Notes

In addition to those mentioned in the references section, the authors would like to extend special thanks to Mr. Chris Marin, human resources director, Sparrow Hospital; Ms. Shirley Stephenson, senior human resource assistant, Sparrow Hospital; and Ms. Catherine Dunn, chairperson, Professional Employees Council of Sparrow Hospital/ Michigan Nurses Association (PECSH/MNA) for their assistance, cooperation, and support in providing access to officials from Sparrow Hospital and PECSH/MNA.

Unless noted parenthetically in the text, the material in this chapter is based on interviews with Aldridge et al. (1999), Barron et al. (1999), Certo et al. (1999), and Daly et al. (1999).

References

Aldridge, Ollie, Kim Alexander, Evelyn Bochenek, George Maier, and Gary McMillan, Sparrow Hospital managers, patient care redesign team members, and bargaining committee members, group interview, 1999.

Barron, Debbie, Dan Phillips, Fran Sklapsky, and Pam Tilton, Sparrow Hospital managers, patient care redesign team members, and bargaining committee members, group interview, 1999.

Certo, Lori, Catherine Dunn, Patricia Frye, Diane Goddeeris, Gail Jehl, Judy McLane, Terri Peaphon, and Jesusa Vasquez, leadership and bargaining committee members of the Professional Employees Council of Sparrow Hospital/Michigan Nurses Association, group interview, 1999.

Daly, Mary Ann, Kim Ford, Jim Fischer, Ira Ginsburg, Gail Grannell, Kathy Kacynski, John Karebian, Rita Michaels, Renee Rivard, Gordon Taylor, and Fred Vocino, members of the Mutual Gains Committee of Sparrow Hospital, group interview, 1999.

Plunkett, Jack. 2000. *Plunkett's Health Care Industry Almanac*. Houston, Texas: Plunkett Research, Ltd.

Strunk, Bradley C., Paul B. Ginsburg, and Jon R. Gabel. 2001. "Tracking Health Care Costs." *Health Affairs* 20(6): 8.

U.S. Bureau of the Census. 1996a. "SU-96-11 Estimates of the Population of Cities with Populations of 10,000 or Greater (Ranked by 1996 Population

Size in State): July 1, 1996." Available at <http://www.census.gov/population/estimates/metro-city/SC1096.txt>.

———. 1996b. "MA-96-5 Estimates of the Population of Metropolitan Areas: Annual Time Series, July 1, 1991 to July 1, 1996." Available at <http://www.census.gov/population/estimates/metro-city/SC10K96.txt>.

9
Overview and Conclusions

Richard N. Block
Michigan State University

As discussed in Chapter 1, the collective bargaining system in the United States is embedded in a belief system that gives great weight to individualism in employment, property rights, and employment solely as a creator of economic value. As compared with the industrial democracies of Europe, the employment relationship is viewed as having very little social content. Whereas in Europe, collectivization of employment as a means of equalizing the influence of employer and employee is the norm, in the United States the norm is an employment relationship between the employer and the individual employee that is based on the economic value each derives from the relationship. Collectivization of employment in the United States does occur but it is not the norm. In 2001, only about 9.7 percent of private-sector employees were covered by collective bargaining agreements (U.S. Bureau of Labor Statistics 2002).

Thus, examining Chapter 2, on the legal, institutional, and economic contexts for collective bargaining, employment protection/creation, and competitiveness, it is not surprising that no actor, institution, or subsystem in the United States encourages the collective bargaining system to be used for those—or any—purposes. Public policy toward employment and collective bargaining, which reflects the individualistic, transactional belief system discussed in Chapter 1, is the most important single influence on the nature of collective bargaining in the United States. With no commitment to a collective bargaining system, public policy neither encourages nor discourages collective bargaining as a method of establishing terms and conditions of employment. Rather, public policy is designed to protect the choice of employees as to whether they wish to be represented by a union/labor organization for the purposes of collective bargaining. Employees make these choices individually, in the privacy of the representation election voting booth. These choices are made on the basis of individual bargaining units, which are legally required to be the employer, plant/facility, or subdivision thereof. In other words, even where employees choose to collectivize, the scope of the collectivity is often quite narrow.

Consistent with the property rights orientation of employment, employers have substantial flexibility in addressing competitiveness through employment system. The unit-by-unit unionization system means that there is no necessary relationship regarding unionization in firm facilities. Thus, it is not unusual for employers to have both unionized and non-union facilities, and to have multiple unions representing employees in the unionized facilities. It may be difficult for unions in different facilities to work together, and it is often very difficult for unions to organize facilities not currently organized (Block, Beck, and Kruger 1996). Employers, through their property rights, have competitiveness options that exclude a union, where one exists, and/or incorporate the potential to require unions to internally compete with one another. The collective bargaining system will be so used to encourage competitiveness and job security/protection only if both parties wish it. If only one party resists, it won't happen. Put differently, labor law simply enables collective bargaining to be used for competitiveness and job security; it does not require or even encourage it to be used for that purpose.

As noted, there is no presumption in U.S. public policy that collective bargaining is a "normal" process of establishing terms and conditions of employment. Rather, "normal" is unilateral employer determination. The underlying assumption is that collective bargaining impairs the ability of firms to compete.[1] A large literature has developed to examine this assumption, and this literature was reviewed in Chapter 3. The discussion in that chapter observed that unions and collective bargaining are more frequently associated with higher productivity and lower production costs than they are with lower productivity and higher production costs, but that unions are associated with reduced profits. There is no evidence that collective bargaining is associated with reduced investment, but there is some evidence that collective bargaining is associated with reduced firm survival. There is no evidence that unionization is also associated with a greater rate of worker displacement among union members. There is some evidence that collective bargaining innovations, such as labor–management cooperation, have a positive effect on product quality, but the effect of

collective bargaining innovations on other measures such as productivity, job security, and training was minimal. Finally, focusing on
employment, where there were employment gains, unionized gains
were lower; where there were employment losses, unionized losses
were greater.

This research suggests the powerful orientation in the United
States toward property rights and the support of labor markets that are
permitted to operate under a transaction assumption with little governmental involvement or employee protection. Under such a system,
unionism and collective bargaining must compete with non-union
employment systems that are closely aligned with the market assumptions of the United States labor market. Thus, it is not surprising that
unions may have some negative employment effects, as firms, using
their property rights, are likely to be tempted to invest less in unionized
facilities than in non-union facilities.

Overall, it appears that much of the presumed impact of unionism
and collective bargaining on firm performance is not borne out by the
research. The effects of unionism are far more complex than would be
believed based on economic theories. This chapter will return to this
theme.

COLLECTIVE BARGAINING, EMPLOYMENT, AND FIRM
PERFORMANCE: PLANT- AND FIRM-LEVEL
PERSPECTIVES

Unlike Chapter 1, which examined collective bargaining at a systemic level, and Chapters 2 and 3, which provided an economy-level
perspective on collective bargaining, Chapters 5–8 took a micro view
by presenting four case studies of the relationship between collective
bargaining, job protection/creation, and firm competitiveness. As discussed in the methodology chapter, Chapter 4, the case studies represented a range of products, production processes, and market
constraints. The four sites studied were Alcoa–Rockdale, Texas, and
United Steelworkers of America Local 4895; General Motors–Lansing,
Michigan, and UAW Local 652; Lear–Elsie, Michigan, and UAW
Local 1660; and Sparrow Health Care Systems, Lansing, Michigan,

and the Michigan Nurses Association. Three were manufacturing sites, and one was a health care service sector site. This section will summarize common themes across all four case studies by examining market issues common to all the cases and differences in how the market affected each firm. The chapter will then summarize the collective bargaining response and provide a brief conclusion.

Market Factors

The employment relationship in the United States is based on value created for the employer. Value in this context is determined primarily by the product market for the good or service produced by the employee. Thus, it is not surprising that a common theme across all the case studies is the importance of the product market as the driver of the collective bargaining relationship. As there are few societally created legislative buffers to insulate the parties from the effects of the product market, the parties in each relationship were required to adjust to the forces affecting the product market for the goods or services produced by the employer and by the workers. In the Alcoa–USW and GM/Lansing–UAW cases, the market forces were direct globalization and increased competition. For the Lear–UAW case, globalization was a level removed, but the cost and quality pressures that the globalized auto industry placed on Lear's customers, the auto manufacturers, were the direct cause of pressure on Lear. In the Sparrow–MNA case, the market pressure came from managed care and the pressure from payers to reduce their insurance outlays. This pressure has caused Sparrow to develop a broad-based strategy of diversification from inpatient care.

In the Alcoa case, the main change in the economic environment was the globalization of the market for aluminum. Whereas for much of the twentieth century Alcoa had been the dominant firm in the aluminum market, able to sets its prices based on cost, this was no longer the case by the late 1980s. The emergence of the London Metal Exchange in the early 1980s, combined with the increased world supply of aluminum, meant that Alcoa was subject to world demand and supply pressures.

Globalization of the market, albeit for automobiles, also affected GM–Lansing and the UAW. It caused GM to lose market share, with a subsequent reorganization that placed plants in competition for product allocation.

Globalization has also encouraged the auto companies to outsource (subcontract) more of their parts work in an effort to reduce costs. This outsourcing was both a threat and an opportunity to a supplier like Lear. While it provided Lear with the opportunity to grow the business, as indicated by employment growth in the industry, the small number of potential purchases and the large size of the purchase also placed extreme cost pressures on Lear in order to obtain that business and to make that business profitable. Sparrow and the Michigan Nurses Association have been required to respond to pressures from the major health care payers and changes in the structure of the health care industry.

Firm-Level Variation

Property rights and the absence of aggregating structures permit firms to create their own responses to market pressures. Thus, the increased market pressure on these relationships had different effects, depending on the firm response. For Alcoa–Rockdale and the USW, the major impact was an increased saliency of the plant's energy cost disadvantage due to its use of coal, forcing the union to reduce labor costs to offset the plant's energy cost disadvantage. For GM–Lansing and UAW Local 652, these pressures manifested themselves in a reorganization by GM. This reorganization forced the Lansing production facilities into the GM allocation system. Thus, the new goal was to encourage GM to allocate the product to Lansing. For Lear, the market pressure is coming from their customers. The market for seat assemblies, while potentially large, is characterized by a small number of potential buyers, namely, those firms in the auto assembly business. The loss of one contract can have a substantial effect on employment. Management and the union must be constantly attentive to this small, identifiable group of customers.

For Sparrow and the MNA, the market pressures are constant. They emanate from the true payers for most health care in the United States, the insurance companies and the government. This cost pressure is placing increased pressure on the traditional resident care business while causing Sparrow to move into tertiary areas, such as outpatient clinics and labs. From a business 20 years ago in which demand was determined by physicians and somebody else paid the bills, Sparrow and the MNA find themselves in a cost-conscious world with a few large buyers.

Collective Bargaining

Despite these differences, all the parties have maintained the traditional written collective bargaining agreement. This structured, legalistic, formal agreement of fixed duration, which explicates the terms and conditions of employment and the rights and obligations of both parties and is enforced by a grievance procedure ending in a final and binding arbitration decision, is the basis of the U.S. system of industrial relations. It is the bedrock on which all of these relationships are based.

At the same time, recognizing the importance of market forces to value-based employment, the parties in these relationships have established joint, extracontractual structures to permit flexibility, with the purpose of maintaining or improving the competitiveness of the facility as the source of maximizing employment. The partnership teams at Alcoa–Rockdale, the "star system" at GM–Lansing, the joint steering teams and planning teams at Lear–Elsie, and the Mutual Gains Committee at Sparrow all represent extracontractual joint activities that were deemed by the parties to be consistent with the collective agreement. It is important to point out, however, that involvement in these joint activities normally represented a willingness by management to cede its rights under the formal collective agreement to make decisions on such matters as how the product or service was produced. It also meant that the union was, for all practical purposes, giving up its right to grieve management decisions, since the decisions made by these extracontractual structures were, in fact, joint decisions rather than management decisions.

Case Study Conclusions

The four case studies presented provide concrete examples of how collective bargaining in the United States can be a vehicle for creating firm competitiveness and employment protection and creation. Despite the variation in the sources of market pressure on these relationships, the parties in all four relationships have developed joint methods of operating. While each structure is specific to the parties' relationship, a common characteristic is a willingness of the firm and the union to put aside their contractual rights and engage in a joint, extracontractual process for competitiveness purposes. Competitiveness, in this context, means success in the product market. Value-based employment requires such success.

Of the four sites, only GM–Lansing and the UAW operate in an environment of some administered job security, through the JOBS program in the GM–UAW national agreement that covers the members of Local 652 and the Lansing site. The JOBS program, however, is designed to prevent layoffs or job reductions associated with increasing productive efficiency, so as to create incentives for GM and the UAW to work jointly to increase competitiveness. It is not a job guarantee in that it does not operate in the event of a volume decline due to market-related conditions. Thus, overall, it is accurate to say that job security in the United States is market-based rather than administered. Consistent with the principle of value-based employment, these four cases have accepted that principle and work within in it.

Given the importance of property rights in the United States, one would expect substantial variation in the structures of these systems, and that is what is seen. The GM–Lansing system is the most formal, with multiple functions reporting to a union joint activities coordinator. Given the size and geographic scope of the GM–Lansing system, this would be expected. Lear and UAW Local 1660 organized its structure, the joint steering team, by function. Sparrow and the Michigan Nurses Association organized the Mutual Gains Committee by the patient care system. Alcoa–Rockdale and the Steelworkers created a structure that was organized by department within a single facility producing aluminum.

These case studies support the conclusions from the review of the literature. Collective bargaining, broadly defined to include not only the formal collective agreement but also joint extracontractual structures, can be a vehicle for both competitiveness and employment protection in the United States. The collective bargaining system in the United States works within the constraints of property-rights-based, value-based employment. Collective bargaining has been successful in promoting these twin goals where the bargaining system has respected the unique characteristics of the production process and the parties to each collective bargaining relationship.

CONCLUSION

Taken together, the overview sections and the case studies reinforce several important themes. First, due to a large extent to the influence of employer property rights, there is wide variation in industrial relations in the United States. This has been documented elsewhere (Block, Beck, and Kruger 1996), and it was reinforced by the case studies here, with the range of options they implemented.

The second important theme is the importance of market-based job security in the United States. The principle of value-based employment means job security comes not from administrative rules in collective bargaining agreements, but from the market success of the firm.

The third important theme is the essential decentralization of collective bargaining in the United States. This is the result of property rights, unit-by-unit bargaining, and local union autonomy.

Fourth, business unionism, as discussed by Perlman ([1928], 1966) has reasserted itself in the United States. There is a narrow local union focus on job security of its members, the incumbents. Given the importance of the job to the worker, it can be argued that principles of union democracy and local union autonomy require a focus on incumbents.

Fifth, and related to the third point above, even in a labor market as strong as that of the United States in the late 1990s, job security is paramount. This demonstrates the importance of the seniority system incorporated in the vast majority of collective bargaining agreements and the continuing existence of a union wage premium, at least for the workers at these sites.

POLICY IMPLICATIONS

The five themes discussed above can be collapsed into two major points that could inform a policy debate regarding the role of collective bargaining in encouraging firm competitiveness and employment protection creation. The first major point is derived from the discussion in Chapter 2 of the institutional framework under which collective bargaining addresses issues of competitiveness and job protection/creation. The second major point is derived from the research on collective bargaining and competitiveness discussed in Chapter 3, and the case studies in Chapters 5–8.

In regard to the institutional framework, public policy views collective bargaining in an employee choice framework, indifferent as to whether there is a strong collective bargaining system. Policy also has little to say about collective bargaining, competitiveness, and employment protection/creation. This follows quite logically from the transaction view of employment. Employment in the United States is a voluntary economic transaction between two individuals with minimal social content. The terms and conditions of employment should be subject to only a minimum of government regulation.

The literature review in Chapter 3 and the case studies in Chapters 5–8 provide a basis for rethinking this view. The literature review in Chapter 3 has shown that research has demonstrated that collective bargaining and firm competitiveness are compatible. Thus, employees can fully participate in their work lives through independent representation, and have industrial democracy, while at the same time encouraging competitiveness in the firms in which they work. The case studies in Chapters 5–8 provided examples of how this compatibility is manifested at the firm or plant level.

Therefore, it may be time for policymakers to rethink the current indifference to collective bargaining as a vehicle for competitiveness, and employment protection/creation, and develop policies that would encourage it. Such policy changes would likely have the advantage of reducing the social costs of unemployment and the disruption associated with the many changes firms must undergo to remain competitive. Employees often have the largest stake in a firm's competitiveness, especially those at the lowest education levels who are the least mobile.

What are possible policy changes? First, the National Labor Relations Act should be amended to make all firm decisions that affect employment, even those that involve a change in the basic nature of the business, subject to collective bargaining. One never knows what suggestions employees will have unless they are given a chance, through their union, to make them. There is no obligation on either side to agree, but what is lost by forcing the parties to bargain about these matters? In addition, making all such decisions negotiable will bring certainty to the law, and will reduce the incentive to litigate over whether a matter should be the subject of negotiations.

Second, the National Labor Relations Board (NLRB) should consider a broader conceptualization of the notion of bargaining unit accretion to permit collective bargaining to be a more viable option than it currently is in questions of intrafirm allocation of resources. For firms with a large number of unionized facilities, the law should decrease the barriers to including in one of those bargaining units a non-union facility that produces a product similar to a proximate and similar unionized facility. Currently, the NLRB permits accretion of a new or acquired facility to an existing bargaining unit based on a consideration of such factors as 1) the degree of interchange of employees among facilities; 2) geographical proximity; 3) integration of operations, machinery, and product lines; 4) centralization of administrative and labor relations control; 5) similarity of working conditions, skills, and job duties; and 6) the number of employees (Harden and Higgins 2001). By giving greater weight to criteria such as product similarity and job duties, and less weight to criteria such as employee interchange and common labor relations control, and by considering proximity less as a criterion for accretion per se and more as a criterion for identifying the host unit, collective bargaining as a vehicle for encouraging firm competitiveness and job security can be strengthened.

Third, Congress should create a permanent labor–management committee to advise it on issues of firm competitiveness and employment protection/creation. Such a committee would not replace the current partisan advocacy through such organizations as the Chamber of Commerce, National Association of Manufacturers, Labor Policy Association, and the AFL-CIO. It would, however, add a new voice to the mix. It would also be a vehicle for labor and management, at a high level, to find common ground. Such a committee would be a mere shadow of the social partnership notion prevalent in Europe, but it would establish the principle of the importance of creating and aggregating labor–management organizations.

These proposals are modest attempts to increase the status of collective bargaining as a tool for encouraging firm competitiveness and job protection/creation. The proposal on expanding the subject matter of bargaining does not change the substantive obligations encompassed in the duty to bargain. The proposal on non-union facilities, while novel, is nothing more than a modification of an established NLRB principle, unit accretion. The proposal on a labor–management committee places no requirement on the committee; rather, it establishes the principle that one should exist. These proposals could be implemented with minimal disruption to the current collective bargaining system in the United States.

Equally important, based on the work shown here, there is no inconsistency between collective bargaining and firm health. Enhancing employee rights in the context of collective bargaining, and supporting collective bargaining, can be obtained at little if any cost to firm competitiveness. In other words, the price of industrial democracy may be much lower than is generally believed.

FINAL OBSERVATIONS

Overall, the work in this book demonstrates that collective bargaining, job protection/creation, and firm competitiveness are compatible in the United States. Employees can enjoy the rights and protections inherent in collective bargaining, and shareholders and other firm stakeholders can prosper. This research has shown that the established view that these are incompatible is at best an oversimplification based on extremely lean economic theories that do not take into account the complexity and flexibility of "real world" employment. At worst, this is a view based on values, ideology, and unstated assumptions. Policymakers concerned about collective bargaining, firm competitiveness, and job protection/creation should understand this as they consider policies in these areas.

Note

1.   An example of this assumption can be found in Schiller (2002).

References

Block, Richard N., John Beck, and Daniel H. Kruger. 1996. *Labor Law, Industrial Relations, and Employee Choice.* Kalamazoo, Michigan: W.E. Upjohn Institute for Employment Research.

Harden, Patrick, and John E. Higgins, eds. 2001. *The Developing Labor Law.* 4th ed. Washington, DC: Bureau of National Affairs.

Perlman, Selig. [1928] 1966. *A Theory of the Labor Movement.* New York: A.M. Kelley.

Schiller, Bradley R. 2002. "Weak Unions Create a Strong Economy." *Wall Street Journal,* January 19.

U.S. Bureau of Labor Statistics. 2002. "Union Members in 2001." News release 02-28, January 17. Available at <http://www.bls.gov/news.release/union2.nr0.htm>.

The Authors

Richard Norman Block is a professor in the School of Labor and Industrial Relations at Michigan State University. He is the author of numerous articles and books on issues in labor and employment law, the relationship between law and practice and industrial relations, industrial relations and structural economic change, employee privacy, international labor standards, and government sponsored employee training. His work has appeared in all major journals in the industrial relations field. He is an experienced labor–management neutral, listed on all major panels, including several private panels.

Dale Belman is an associate professor in the School of Labor and Industrial Relations at Michigan State University, where he teaches economics and statistics. His areas of research include collective bargaining and the effect of regulation on the performance of firms and labor markets. He has coauthored *How New is the 'New Employment Contract'?* and *Sailors of the Concrete Sea: The Work and Work Life of Truck Drivers*. His research has appeared in the *Review of Economics and Statistics, Industrial and Labor Relations Review, Industrial Relations, Empirical Economics, Public Finance Review* and *Oxford Economic Papers*.

Peter Berg is an associate professor at the School of Labor and Industrial Relations at Michigan State University. He received his Ph.D. in economics from the University of Notre Dame. He recently coauthored the book *Manufacturing Advantage: Why High Performance Work Systems Pay Off*, from Cornell/ILR University Press, 2000.

Michael L. Moore is a professor at the School of Labor and Industrial Relations at Michigan State University, where he teaches graduate-level courses in High Performance Work Systems and Compensation and Benefits Systems. He received his Ph.D. at the University of Michigan. Dr. Moore served as director of the School of Labor and Industrial Relations from 1993–1998. His current research focus is the role of human resources and labor relations systems in lean manufacturing environments.

Michael Polzin is an assistant professor in the School of Labor and Industrial Relations at Michigan State University. His work is primarily with the Program on Innovative Employment Relations Systems (PIERS), an outreach unit of the school that works only with unionized organizations to facilitate joint labor–management change initiatives. Prior to joining the school, Mike worked on staff with the National Union of Hospital and Health Care Employees, District 1199C, and with a Philadelphia-based consulting group that created unionized, worker-owned businesses.

Index

The italic letters *f*, *n*, and *t* following a page number indicate that the subject information is within a figure, note, or table, respectively, on that page.

163

About the Institute

The W.E. Upjohn Institute for Employment Research is a nonprofit research organization devoted to finding and promoting solutions to employment-related problems at the national, state, and local levels. It is an activity of the W.E. Upjohn Unemployment Trustee Corporation, which was established in 1932 to administer a fund set aside by the late Dr. W.E. Upjohn, founder of The Upjohn Company, to seek ways to counteract the loss of employment income during economic downturns.

The Institute is funded largely by income from the W.E. Upjohn Unemployment Trust, supplemented by outside grants, contracts, and sales of publications. Activities of the Institute comprise the following elements: 1) a research program conducted by a resident staff of professional social scientists; 2) a competitive grant program, which expands and complements the internal research program by providing financial support to researchers outside the Institute; 3) a publications program, which provides the major vehicle for disseminating the research of staff and grantees, as well as other selected works in the field; and 4) an Employment Management Services division, which manages most of the publicly funded employment and training programs in the local area.

The broad objectives of the Institute's research, grant, and publication programs are to 1) promote scholarship and experimentation on issues of public and private employment and unemployment policy, and 2) make knowledge and scholarship relevant and useful to policymakers in their pursuit of solutions to employment and unemployment problems.

Current areas of concentration for these programs include causes, consequences, and measures to alleviate unemployment; social insurance and income maintenance programs; compensation; workforce quality; work arrangements; family labor issues; labor-management relations; and regional economic development and local labor markets.

DATE DUE

1/9/06			

Printed
in USA